THE OPEN MIND
GUEST LECTURES

1989 – 1998

THE OPEN MIND GUEST LECTURES

1989 – 1998

editor
John Quinn

First published 1999
by the Institute of Public Administration,
57-61 Lansdowne Road,
Dublin, Ireland.

British Library Cataloguing in Publication Data

ISBN 1 902448 08 1

Cover design by Creative Inputs, Dublin
Typeset by Fingers Unltd., Dublin
Printed by ColourBooks, Dublin

Contents

Réamhrá

Le deich mbliana anuas, thug Aoi-Léacht an *Open Mind* ardán craolta do chainteoirí céimiúla. Tugadh cuireadh dóibh labhairt ar ábhair dá rogha féin. Mar thoradh ar sin, thug deich gcláracha de chraoladh spreagúil raidió dúshlán d'éisteoirí chun ath-mhachnamh a dhéanamh ar raon leathan de cheisteanna chomhaimseartha – polaitíocht, eacnamaíocht, oideachas, beatha an anama agus cumhacht na leabhar ina measc. D'fhéadfaí a rá i dtaobh na léachtaí seo go léir go mbaineann siad le cothú na muintire i gcomhthéacs síochána agus sibhialtachta.

Gach bliain, caitear cuid mhór de chraoladh RTÉ, mar chraoltóir náisiúnta, ar thaifeadadh na staide ina bhfuilimid. Is minic súil siar againn ar an staid ina rabhamar agus ar an mbóthar a ghabhamar go dtí an lá atá inniu ann. Agus ar uaire – sna léachtaí seo, cur i gcás – spreagann ár gcraoladh sinn chun aghaidh a thabhairt ar a bhfuil romhainn. Taispeántar roghanna éagsúla a bheidh ar fáil, ceistítear ár réamhchlaonta agus ár réamhthuairimí. Thar aon ní eile, bíonn fiafraí agus síorchuardach le brath.

Táimid buíoch de na léachtóirí as a bhflaithiúlacht aigne agus meoin. Cuireann sé áthas ar leith orm fáiltiú roimh an bhfoilseachán seo mar thaifead ar a ndúradar, agus mar fhianaise ar an gcuma a ndeineann craolachán na seirbhíse poiblí a chuid féin chun an plé bunúsach a spreagadh i measc an phobail.

Bob Collins,
Príomh-Stiúrthóir RTÉ

Foreword

For the past ten years, the *Open Mind Guest Lecture* has offered a broadcast platform to distinguished speakers, with an invitation to speak on subjects of their own choosing. As a result, ten stimulating radio programmes have challenged listeners to think again about a wide ambit of contemporary affairs, including politics, economics, education, the life of the spirit and the power of the book. One way of describing the common concern of these lectures is to say that they are about the work of building up our human community in peace and civility.

Every year RTÉ, as the national broadcasting service, devotes much of its output to recording the state we are in. Frequently, we look back at the way we were, and the road we travelled to reach the present. And sometimes – as in these lectures – our broadcasting prompts us to explore the future. It offers us alternatives and options; it questions our prejudices and our assumptions. Above all, it conveys a sense of seeking.

We are grateful to the lecturers for their generosity of mind and spirit. I am particularly pleased to welcome this publication both as a record of their spoken words, and as evidence of how public service broadcasting plays its part in furthering vital debate in our society.

Bob Collins,
Director-General RTÉ

Introduction

In October 1989, to mark ten years of the radio programme *Education Forum*, I organised a lecture series on the theme 'Education for the 1990s'. Three speakers addressed that theme from varying perspectives: Dr John Coolahan, Professor of Education at St Patrick's College, Maynooth, presented an overview of the educational landscape with regard to formal schooling; Ann Higgins, a primary teacher and founder of 'The Three O'Clock School' in Killeely, Limerick, released a barrage of hard-hitting questions about the nature and focus of our education system; Professor Mike Cooley, consultant, writer and broadcaster on work and technology, outlined the courage and imagination that will be required to face the new millennium.

The lectures were subsequently broadcast on *The Open Mind* (successor to *Education Forum*), to much acclaim. The audience reaction prompted the idea of an annual public lecture by a guest speaker, on a topic of the speaker's choosing. Thus was born the *Open Mind Guest Lecture*.

Entering the final decade of the century tends to focus minds on aspirations for a new century. James Robertson, a much-respected independent writer and thinker, faced up to that task in the 1990 *Open Mind Guest Lecture* when his theme was 'Health, Wealth and Wisdom for the 21st Century'. For the past twenty years, James Robertson has been calling for a new path of progress, based on co-operative self-reliance rather than on domination and dependency.

Increasing urbanisation and the gradual erosion of the agriculture industry caused Michael Cuddy to pose a timely question in the 1991 *Guest Lecture*. 'What future for rural Ireland?' was Michael's question and, from his perspective as a Professor of Economics in University College Galway, he was in an excellent position to offer a challenging and sobering answer.

Michael D Higgins was our guest speaker in 1992, and in a paper entitled 'Education for Freedom', he made a passionate plea for a Great Education Debate. Drawing on his own experience of education, Michael D Higgins (whose appointment as Minister for Arts, Culture and the Gaeltacht was then imminent) made a further plea for a pedagogy of love rather than a pedagogy of fear ...

Love was very much the theme of the 1993 *Open Mind Guest Lecture*. 'The bottom line is love' was Gordon Wilson's favourite expression. His 'wee story from Enniskillen' (not *the* story, but *a* story, he was at pains to point out) was not so much a lecture, more a personal journey – harrowing, deeply moving and totally uplifting. When the evening's proceedings ended, no one in the audience moved for a few minutes. 'Just give us time to compose ourselves,' one of them pleaded.

Gordon Wilson told his 'wee story' on a historic night in 1993 – December 15th, the date of the Downing Street Declaration, the first chink of hope in the Peace Process. The chink widened in 1994, when Republican and Loyalist ceasefires were declared. It seemed an apt time to invite one of the principal architects of the Peace Process – John Hume – to deliver the *Open Mind Guest Lecture*. His title was simple and self-explanatory and was at the core of his long, untiring struggle to bring peace to Northern Ireland – 'Leaving the Past Behind' ...

1995 marked the fiftieth anniversary of the founding of the United Nations, an organisation that had achieved much in those fifty years and yet had also attracted no small measure of criticism. It was time to make an honest appraisal of the role of the UN. Cometh the hour, cometh the man! Erskine Childers (the third generation to bear that distinguished name in Irish life) had recently retired, following a notable career in the service of the United Nations. He readily agreed to give the 1995 *Open Mind Lecture* on the theme 'The United Nations in the Real World' – a frank, hard-hitting appraisal of the structure and operation of the organisation Erskine Childers knew so well. The lecture rekindled Erskine's love for an earlier career – broadcasting – and he returned to it with enthusiasm before his sudden death in 1996.

The rapid advances in technology, particularly in the areas of communication and entertainment, have raised questions about the future of the book. Can it survive as a source of information and/or entertainment? Award-winning author Anne Fine, who writes for both children and adults, took up the challenge of answering that question in the 1996 *Open Mind Guest Lecture* entitled 'Open Book, Open Mind – Why We Read Books and Why We Need Them'. Anne made the case for the book in a witty, finely argued and hugely entertaining talk.

A phenomenon of the publishing industry in recent years has been the plethora of books on spirituality – witness the size of the 'Mind, Body, Spirit' section in any decent bookstore. In Ireland, the book-publishing success of 1997 was *Anam Chara*, John O'Donohue's reflections on Celtic Spirituality. When I invited John to give the 1997 *Guest Lecture*, he chose the intriguing title 'Towards a Philosophy of Absence'. Before a capacity audience, John explored the many-faceted concept of absence in the true style of a philosopher-poet.

And so to 1998. The great story of the year has been the Good Friday Agreement, hopefully the resolution of a thirty-year nightmare in Northern Ireland. For the past three years, the fragile Peace Process has been steered through the rockiest of waters by one man in particular – Senator George Mitchell.

Following a distinguished legal and senatorial career in the United States, his choice as Chairman of the multiparty peace negotiations in Northern Ireland was an inspired one. His patience and tenacity of purpose in seeing those negotiations through to fruition will leave generations, north and south, deeply in his debt.

I am personally indebted to him and very deeply honoured that he should give the 1998 *Open Mind Guest Lecture* on the theme 'Towards Peace in Northern Ireland'. It is a fitting culmination of ten years of quality broadcasting which has enriched the ferment of ideas on a broad range of important topics.

John Quinn

At the 1994 *Open Mind Guest Lecture*:
John Hume (1994 Speaker), John Quinn (Producer),
Gordon Wilson (1993 Speaker)

1989

THEME

EDUCATION FOR THE 1990s

SPEAKERS

John Coolahan
Professor of Education, St Patrick's College, Maynooth

Mike Cooley
*Engineer, trade unionist, broadcaster, writer
and consultant on human-centred technology*

Ann Higgins
*Primary teacher, community worker and founder of
'The Three O'Clock School', Killeely, Limerick*

Dr John Coolahan

Introduction

Looking to the future is usually a mixture of wishful thinking – what one hopes will happen and what is likely to happen. I suppose it is part of the buoyancy of being human to hope for progress, to aspire to reform – although of course it is very often to indulge too much in Utopian fantasy. However, by lifting one's sights to envisage what might be possible, one can help in the process of making it possible. The influence of precedent, of past experience, of strong traditions, can be enabling in planning appropriate reform, but it can also be a mental straitjacket. We've become so accustomed to the status quo that we find it very difficult to envisage significant movement from it. But I think we, in our generation, would be culpably ignorant to fall into that trap, because one of the great privileges of being alive in the second half of the twentieth century is the extent and pace of change in political, social, economic, technological and communications activity.

The 1980s

In any reflection on the way forward, I think it is important to touch a little on lines of continuity that lead us into that arena. As we peered into the future here in RTÉ in 1979, the areas of predicted concern in fact proved largely accurate. But the pattern of their handling turned out to be very different and some elements were not foreseen, or were very much underestimated; in particular, the very steep decline in birthrate was not predicted, nor was the full depth of the economic recession.

The 1980s could be characterised as a decade of great upheaval and frustration in education circles. The first two years of the decade saw as many as six Ministers for Education changing places. Mass marches and rallies of teachers took place on the streets; parents also became militant and made their views on educational cutbacks very clear to politicians.

Ireland was by no means unique in this; many countries cut back on educational expenditure, sometimes with more devastating impact than in the case of Ireland. We are too close to the events to establish good historical perspective, but interesting and promising features also occurred. Despite all the difficulties, the reality remained that massive expansion continued in our pupil population, particularly at second and third level. The general levels of student retention and educational achievement have been very striking. We can again aspire to the description of an island of scholars, although the associated phrase, an island of saints, is much more problematic.

One large college of education was closed down, arousing much controversy, but the last year of the decade saw the State establish its first universities. The establishment of the National Parents' Council in 1985 was symbolic of a more central role for parents within the system – an agency which is likely to become much more prominent in the 1990s. It has been a decade of remarkable appraisal of the system. A range of representative committees set up by the Minister for Education reported on such issues as Educational Broadcasting, Adult Education, In-service Education for Teachers, School Discipline, and so on. Part of the frustration arose from the lack of implementation of such reports, coinciding as they did with the crisis in the public finances. The decade opened with the state's first ever *White Paper on Education* in 1980, followed in January 1984 with the government's *Programme for Action* – also a type of White

Paper. In 1985, the government announced its rather short-lived decisions on *The Ages for Learning*, while in the same year the state's first Green Paper on Education, *Partners in Education*, was published.

In 1984, the Curriculum and Examinations Board (CEB) was established and replaced by the National Council for Curriculum and Assessment (NCCA) in 1987. Also in 1987, the Primary Curriculum Review Body was set up, and in 1988 the overall Review Body on Primary Education came into being. In 1986, the Organisation for Economic Co-operation and Development (OECD) was invited by the government to report on Irish education, with special reference to teacher education.

There are two ways of looking at all this analysis and reportage. One could consider these as occasions for letting off steam, talking shops, mechanisms for delaying decisions, or one could see them as valuable opportunities which examine the many features of the system and which provide a good foundation on which policy for the 1990s can be based, when circumstances may be more favourable for developmental action. One could also hold a bit of both viewpoints: recognising the delaying tactic aspect, but also recognising that some developmental initiatives may emerge from the analyses.

It is also the case that, if action is not taken on these reports, we will have laid the seeds of a very bad harvest. A further layer of cynicism will be trowelled on – something we could do without. A very great deal of voluntary effort was forthcoming in the various working committees, often by overworked people, and a system which insults that commitment by consigning such reports to dusty pigeonholes as historical curiosities will have undermined much that is valuable in the concept of public service.

On the other hand, the nature of the participation of interested parties preparing, earlier on in the 1980s, the

Programme for Action, and participating in groups mentioned – the CEB, the NCCA and the various review bodies – could have much promise for the '90s. Teachers, parents and managements have participated alongside departmental staff. There is a widening of perspective, a learning process involved for all parties, and a feeling of being involved in the forging of educational policy.

In a system as centralised as Ireland's, this process could be very productive and could subtly reshape the nature of policy-making and the interrelationship between involved parties over the years ahead.

The 1990s

When one looks a little bit more precisely towards the '90s, two factors which were underestimated ten years ago, namely the pupil population and the economic situation, are set to have a huge bearing on developments now. When the increases in population from the early '60s were combined with the policy of expanding access to and duration of schooling, resources were greatly stretched to cope with the quantitative expansion. Now that scenario has changed. During the '90s, we will be catering for a greatly reduced school-pupil clientele. The national economic situation which was in the doldrums and at zero growth levels for many years is now firmly predicted to grow by 5.7% per annum in a sustained way up towards 1993 – insofar as economists are firm about anything. I think this reminds us of the era of the early '60s, when annual growth rates were 4.5% for a sequence of years, and that was the time which fuelled the great reform of Irish education.

This combination of factors (reduced pupil population and greatly improved economic performance) could provide the circumstances for a great drive forward in improving the quality of Irish education, if there is good analysis, good planning, good co-operation and good leadership. One would hope that the Department of Education itself will be a little bit more selfish in the sense that it will seek to have itself more satisfactorily resourced to fulfil the multifaceted range of responsibilities thrust upon it. It would also be desirable that the forms of partnership in planning which we've touched on in the '80s would be fostered and developed, either through regional education authorities or through consultative structures. The experience, wisdom and aspiration of professional and parental interests should be drawn upon and channelled into productive and 'involving' aspects of education policy-making.

Demographic Change

One of the most obvious changes in the educational landscape at the end of the next decade will be the reduction in the number of schools to be observed thereon. The demographic realities now require and will require closures and amalgamations at post-primary as well as at primary school level. A further striking feature of our schooling system (particularly at secondary level) for almost two centuries also seems set to change greatly by the end of the next decade. I refer to the role of the religious. What is referred to (and I don't mean this disrespectfully) as the thinning and greying of the religious will greatly alter their traditional involvement in education. This trend is also coinciding with some fundamental reappraisal by them of the nature of their role in vocational emphasis within changing societal needs.

As you know, we have a large stock of post-primary schools which belong to different managements and trustees, and many of these schools are competing in local catchment areas. A new edge to that competition is likely to develop with schools facing declining enrolments in the '90s; in fact, that 'new edge' is already with us. Important decisions will need to be made about school closures, amalgamations and the development of staff and this calls for leadership, diplomacy and flexibility from the key parties involved. In this context, on behalf of the common good and in the cause of efficiency and equity, it is very desirable that the state, in my view, should promote and guide the orderly provision of a post-primary schooling system, either through central control or through the setting up of regional educational authorities. Individual school managements need to show flexibility and be concerned about the best educational outcomes for the pupils in their catchment areas, but – and this is very important – they need assistance and facilitation to help them through difficult transitional times. Already many of them on the ground have achieved a great deal, but sometimes the copper-fastening of agreements which have been reached has been withheld because of the unavailability of capital resources that would have taken the thing forward and broken the log-jam. This is unquestionably, I think, one of the key issues facing us in the '90s and the dangers of mishandling it are huge. The danger in local communities of teachers against teachers, and parents opposed to parents – with the general fabric of our local communities being damaged – is very serious and one hopes that the rather laid-back attitude taken by a significant number of responsible agents at the moment may not be indulged in for too long more, and that a more pro-active facilitatory process may be drawn upon.

A consolation in relation to the reduction in the number of schools may well be, of course, the opportunity to improve the provision of resources in the schools that remain. Now, as well as fewer, but one hopes better-equipped, schools, the pressure is on to change what we do in schools and how we do it. More of the same is not sufficient. And here it strikes me that three elements at the cutting edge of the teaching-learning encounter – the curriculum, the method of pedagogy and the modes of assessment – are terribly closely interrelated and each of them requires great and contemporaneous attention. They also need to be rooted in sound educational principles, rather than responding to pressure groups or ephemeral fads. The question of curriculum change is an issue that has been with us since the mid-60s, and it is an ongoing pattern rather than something novel to be worried about in the '90s. In many ways, within the context of the expansion of schooling in Ireland over the recent decades, both primary and post-primary schools have been much more innovative in curricular areas than they are generally given credit for. Nevertheless, the move to universal post-primary schooling with its very heterogeneous clientele, as well as many deep societal and cultural changes, emphasise the continuing need to adapt, update and innovate in areas of school curricula.

Curriculum

One of the things we predicted ten years ago was that the momentum was such that curriculum change had to break through very early in the '80s. It is a bit discouraging that it took a decade before more significant progress was made – though a good deal of reflective work was done through the CEB and the NCCA. In the autumn of 1989, we have a significant visible development – the Junior Cycle syllabuses. And the hope is that they will move forward towards Senior Cycle as we move into the '90s. They are a visible evidence of much of the homework or the groundwork coming to fruition.

One needs to watch central things within our curricular change at the moment, because we are part of a very key transitional phase in Irish education. We also need to watch something we give a lot of verbal allegiance to, but do not work very hard to implement – and that is the sense of balance in the curriculum. Right from the start of the state, we gave verbal allegiance to the idea of a balanced liberal education. But, in practice, the cognitive and intellectual have dominated the experience of most of our children, and in particular the arts, physical education, and some aspects of social education have been significantly neglected. One would hope that in the provision for the '90s, we commit ourselves to work harder to achieve that better balance, because of the centrality of the issues involved and the key importance for the young children who are our significant responsibility.

In relation to curricular reform, we are very impatient about giving in-depth thought in advance to the implementation process. It is much more difficult than preparing the documents, requiring much more patience and much more guts to think it through. Regrettably, one has to record that, in the present instance of the Junior Cycle, the processes of implementation leave a very great deal to be desired.

Pedagogy

Linked to the desire for curricular change at all levels is a key concern for a form of pedagogy which is more varied, imaginative, integrating and challenging. It is desired not just by ourselves. It is part of a pattern internationally to encourage greater individualisation of the learning process, with less didactic teaching and much greater direct pupil involvement in and responsibility for his or her own learning. What we need to try to work at is to remove the sometimes passive or routine participation of pupils, so that they may be more activated with high quality teacher/pupil interaction. But high quality pedagogy also has cost implications, particularly in the areas of pupil/teacher ratios and in-service education for teachers. There is a third part of this central issue in education. Curricular and pedagogic changes need to be matched by the appropriate assessment procedures. Again, I stress they need to be thought about contemporaneously in the planning stages.

Assessment

The very heavy burden placed on the examinations as selecting mechanisms of our society at the moment sends tension right through the schooling systems. The high levels of competitiveness do, of course, act as a strong deterrent to teachers in taking more adventurous pedagogic pathways, even when they know that that is the right thing to do. Unless the examination process is adapted to suit the favoured styles of teaching and to curricular content, teachers will, in fact, be reluctant to depart from methods geared to success in the traditional examinations. This, of course, presents a very great challenge to those in charge of examinations and in that area of assessment I would say we're almost primitive in our thinking. We expect hard-pressed inspectors of the various subjects to work long, hard hours, night and day, to try to put together assessment procedures. If we are serious about assessment and moving it forward, we need to finance a group of people who can go at it full-time, who can pilot things, who can build up data banks, who can test and re-test and get things going, and draw on other resources and other advice.

So the three things are interlocked and I leave it there, except to say that I think we would be very naïve to think that there are going to be tremendous moves in that direction. I think it is going to be very much a process of what we've had already – of slow, gradual edging forward. The danger I would see is that, whatever about getting out curricula, the pedagogic situation will settle into much more of the same, and the assessment procedures will endorse that. There's a much greater job afoot than I think has been centrally taken on board, and I think that has been the problem right from the early '80s with the CEB. If you are going to shift the curricula of schools, the style of teaching in schools and the modes of assessment in schools you have about one of the most difficult jobs a nation can ever undertake. There is a whole host and cluster of dependent variables in there, and if you are going to bring them with you, the minimum you need is to have this taken on board as a government issue, not a Minister's issue. It needs to be seen on an inter-sectoral basis, where, in particular, the Departments of Finance, Industry and Commerce, Labour and, indeed to some extent, Environment too, see themselves as rowing in behind, in a team effort. Whether Education likes that or not – insofar as all the old traditional demarcations are very real things – is, I think, neither here nor there. Lots of us have to cope with things we don't like. But it appears to me that the process is likely to be a slow, gradual, stop/go kind of effort – nevertheless, it will probably shift and, after ten years, one hopes it will have shifted a good bit.

Europe

Another obvious dimension that we're going to experience in the next number of years is, of course, the whole European dimension. Ireland opens up the new decade in January with the Presidency of the European Commission, as represented by our Taoiseach, and I think this is a striking reminder to us of how much the decade is expected to enhance greater European integration with 1992 and all that. One of the striking aspects of our involvement with the EC since our accession is the very positive attitude towards European movement among the general public in Ireland, and interestingly, this is also reflected in the ESRI survey on pupil and teacher attitudes early in 1989, following the *Europe in the Classrooms* project. It is quite remarkable how favourable teachers' and pupils' attitudes were towards concepts of Europe.

We've already seen the strength of the European link in the resources of VPT, in the tremendous resourcing that is going into training programmes in the regional technical colleges and in the *School to Work* projects. The new programmes, *Erasmus*, *Comet*, *Lingua* and *Petra*, and the Youth Exchange Programmes are likely to be very much more heard of in the '90s. The curricular implications will vary and I think the NCCA are correct not to move towards the idea of a European Studies component, but to work more towards infusion, towards the question of history, geography and the various subjects taking on a European orientation and perspective. Obviously, the stress will be on European languages, and we will have to address them more seriously.

But one also hopes that our greater links with Europe may open people's minds to the impact of the European school resource and what we are doing with our resources in relation to what they are doing with theirs. One thing that strikes me very much, as I reflect on Ireland and Europe, and read up a little bit from time to time, is the commonality of the problems in different countries. There is a remarkable similarity in the underlying problems being encountered by school systems internationally at the moment.

The School Ethos

Again, linking internationally, I think there is a movement afoot (and I think it's a very wise one for educators to take on board here) to urge the schools to take a more overt concern and recognition within the schools themselves of establishing a school community ethos, which would include the process of whole school planning and close teamwork among the school personnel as they articulate, shape and implement the educational policies of their schools. As we know, the second level school has got within it the vast majority now of young people between the ages of twelve to eighteen. I don't think we have adapted sufficiently to this clientele. I think schools would be wise to concentrate a good deal on the quality of the interpersonal relationships within the schools in the '90s; the respect for the attitudes of pupils, the understanding and awareness of the socioeconomic, domestic and peer pressures on adolescents, and how the hidden curriculum as well as the formal curriculum and the styles of teaching, modes of assessment and pupil feedback really need very careful planning if we are going to respond satisfactorily to these young people in relation to their integrity as people. We have made it compulsory for them to attend school up to fifteen and have indirectly made it compulsory for them to come much longer and much later. Accordingly, there is a moral responsibility on us to ensure that we provide worthwhile, interesting and satisfying experiences for them.

Now, as well as the school focusing more on itself and becoming in a way more introverted, there is a linked dimension which I think is a pattern that will evolve more in the '90s. We brought it in very interestingly in the concept of the Community School in 1970, and in some ways it has evolved – so it wouldn't be a totally new phenomenon. It is a question of building on ongoing trends, but of doing so in a more concentrated and a more conscious way, and that is the development of the school within its community – we've talked about the school as a community but, likewise, the school within and linked into its community. Now here, I think, the possibilities of school/work links, work experience situations and leisure and outward bound activities, linking in to the environment, etc., can have tremendous potential.

Continuing Education

For a long time now, the realisation has been there and we've had an awful lot of ink spilled, indicating to us that formal education is not something that should be confined to one's youth, but that continuing education is highly desirable for personal, vocational and social reasons in a society undergoing such fundamental and rapid change. However, for many of those most in need, the resources and facilitation for continuing and adult education have remained inadequate and obdurately so. Worthwhile initiatives towards mature students and forms of distance education hopefully will get greater support in the years to come, because undoubtedly the societal needs of the day do require further education, second-chance education and retraining. These will be crucial for large groups of people or else we will seriously impede their sense of self-satisfaction, their realisation of their potential as people in the one single experience of living they are ever going to get.

Many agencies, I think, are now in place with experience, insights and expertise in the area of adult education, so let it be well targeted, well devised and not a loose amorphous well-meaning thing. Can we build upon that, and can we direct some of the resources which we hope will be released towards improving the co-ordination between them, putting adult education into a stronger position by the end of the next decade? Again, I suppose there's more aspiration than confidence in that. I don't think past experience can allow anybody to be very confident that we will go far down that road, but I suppose I could be wrong there.

Third Level Education

What has been achieved over the last two decades in the variety of third level institutions, and the extraordinary range and multiplicity of courses that are available within all the institutions collectively, is quite frankly something of a remarkable achievement that we take for granted too easily. Provision of expensive third level places for the huge bulge of second level pupils is causing us great difficulties at present, and you know the hassle and the publicity and the problems over the summer on points and matrics and what-have-you. There is no doubt at all that this has to be one of the great challenges of the '90s for us. It is already with us – it was a great challenge in the '80s. And even though there will, in the long run, be a follow-through in regard to birthrate decline and that will gradually work its way to third level, the situation in the new century is unlikely to be easier because I think rising social demand and aspiration for third level places will ensure that the demand is sustained. One sees very little chance of accommodating many more students into existing short and crowded courses in institutions already at their wits' end coping with greater demands, but with reduced resources.

Here I think a word of caution needs to be exercised: we could be in danger of making an extraordinary mistake by putting the final straw on that camel's back. Particularly within the NUI framework, we are now operating degree courses in, say Arts in some subjects on a two-and-a-half year basis, and what's more, honours degree courses on a two-and-a-half year basis – frequently in very large classes with inadequate tutorial resources. Now you can go down that road for a while, but you are quite surely going to end up in a cul-de-sac, because the slippage in standards and in the respect for our qualifications internationally, which have been very painfully built up with a lot of effort, would be seriously in jeopardy. When one hears politicians and other commentators speaking about 4-term years and so on, I really feel they are at a distant remove from the coalface.

Hopefully the new communications media can be brought to bear, but that's a very expensive process in a small society like ours, if we're going to do it out of our own indigenous cultural resources. We can buy in some, but I think there are dangers in buying in all.

New institutional alignments may be in the offing and it is conceivable that, while we began 1989 with two universities in Ireland, we could well have seven universities by 1999.

Teachers

When it comes down to it, the core of the whole system – the core element of any attempt to improve and to move in these pathways into the '90s – will reside in the quality and calibre of the teachers. And there is no gainsaying that without an intelligent, well-trained, imaginative and committed teaching force, campaigns and paper programmes for greater quality in the educational system will fail to meet their objectives. Many of the desired reforms involve great demands on the role of the teacher as professional and the flight from teaching that has occurred internationally may very well take root here.

The centrality of the teacher's role is being re-emphasised as the school casts its influence over more human beings for longer periods of their lives than ever before in human history.

Strangely enough, Ireland could be very well positioned in this regard because it has to hand a magnificent teaching force. I've said this on a few other occasions but I genuinely believe it – that one of the great fortunes of Ireland has been the quality and calibre of the teachers attracted into the system, not the largesse of institutional resources. We may be in danger – linked to declining job opportunities but more potently, or at least as potently, attitudinal issues within society – of letting that slip. On the other hand, if the resources can be targeted, and significant and realistic planning put into effect, we may be able to do something that could be remarkable in building on the tradition of teaching within Irish educational history – and that is something we could never have done up to now, because of the need to man the overstretched system. What we can do now, however, is to take on board seriously the 'three Is' concept – improving *initial*, *induction* and *in-service* education.

The numbers now in initial teacher education have declined significantly, allowing for a much more qualitative handling of it; the induction process may be very bric-a-brac now in terms of job opportunities but nevertheless could be very much improved and then you're going nowhere unless you can manage to in-build periodically significant forms of in-service training of a varied kind. Whether we do it or not is again open to question, and it is of course easy when you aren't in the Department of Finance to say these things. Nevertheless, it will cost a certain amount to do, but any economist or Department of Finance official would be terribly foolish if they didn't realise what a cost it's going to be if we don't do it.

In 1979, I thought teacher unity among the unions was much more likely to come earlier in the '80s than it did in fact do. In ways it came, and you got the Council of Education Unions and you got the combined groups in Croke Park on the arbitration problems and so on, but somehow or another, the unions haven't pulled it together. I think there is an extraordinary urgency in that myself; I feel there's a big changing scenario to come in the '90s and that there is a tremendous amount of value to be gained by a unified teaching force facing new opportunities and new challenges.

Conclusion

The twin goals, it appears to me, that we need in the '90s are to watch for the quality of our educational system and to watch that we sustain the motivation of key agents within the system, and I think it is an issue which is very fundamental to the ongoing quality of our society at large. I think it calls for an intersectoral social strategy in the planning stages. It needs to be part of national programme planning so that a range of social partners – their activities and resources – can be harnessed to the cause. Why should we try to work hard at trying to achieve that? Because, I think, of the centrality of the issues involved in the wellbeing of democratic society in Ireland in the late twentieth century and beyond.

Dr Mike Cooley

It is not my intention to deliver a highly structured lecture on education in the 1990s. To do so would be to repeat here the mistake which, in my view, is at the very root of our western society at this historical stage – that of over-structuring. We've over-structured everything to such an extent that we've suppressed imagination, creativity, ingenuity and the sheer sense of fun and excitement which comes from discovery.

Education, in my view, has been so over-structured in western society, in particular in the United Kingdom, that it has now degenerated into mere instruction, or even worse perhaps, into arid training. Training is a narrow machine- or system-specific competence which is obsolete the moment the system ceases to exist. And given the range of technological change and the incredible rate of that change, much of that training is obsolete in two or three years' time.

Education is a more durable quality. It is, as one of my German colleagues put it to me, a state of mind. My hierarchy of verbs in these matters would be that you *programme* a robot, an athlete and possibly a soldier, you *train* a dog, and you *provide educational environments* for human beings. If you suspect that this is an exaggeration, I have to tell you that there are now already computer models which organise universities as factories. The system talks about 'student processing' in the same way we might talk about car components. In the software, the students are referred to as 'commodities', the examinations as 'quality control procedures', graduation as 'delivery' and the professors as 'operators'. And they use a Frank-Wolfe algorithm to work out the rate at which the professors are thinking. The last thing

we will require in the 1990s will be these clone-like figures
now being pressed out of our educational system.

What we will require is people, whether they've been to
university or not, who are sensitive to the growing catastrophe
that is building up in our environmental and social structures.
And we will require people with imagination and energy to do
something about it.

The 1990s are the last ten years of building blocks before
the 21st century. In a narrow reductionist sense, the year 2000
can be seen as simply 1999 plus 1. It could also be viewed by
reductionists as 2001 minus 1. For me, however, it is the end
of an extraordinary millennium, a millennium which has seen
the growth of our modern cities, the decline of feudalism, the
growth of capitalism, the Renaissance, and above all, the
development of our Cartesian form of western science and
technology. The notion of the 21st century, it seems to me,
will provide a powerful psychological impetus in which to
question where we are going. And to do that, we will need
people with the courage to ask why it is that we've developed
forms of agricultural production so energy- and chemically-
intensive that in France, milk from a mother's breast is so
polluted that it would be illegal to sell it in a bottle. Within the
next century alone, we will reduce the number of species of
fauna and flora by fifty percent. We will destroy half the species
of plants and animals we now see about us. And not only are
we doing that to nature – we are doing the same sort of things
to ourselves.

Why is it that we deploy our resources in this way? How is
it that we produce missile systems that can guide a missile to
another continent with an accuracy of a few millimetres, when
the blind and the disabled still stagger round our cities in very
much the same way as they did in medieval times? Why is it
that we allow this form of science and technology to bludgeon
our common sense into silence? And this technology and science
so intrudes into all areas of our lives that we feel diminished

and degraded by it. In the field of expert systems, they are now developing systems which not only will emulate human beings; they will, in their view, replace them. According to some colleagues at Stanford, 'human beings will have to accept their true place in the evolutionary hierarchy, namely, animals, human beings and intelligent machines'. We are going to require people – they may not be educated in the usual sense – who will need to have the common sense to say that a microphone is not an ear, a camera is not an eye, and a computer is not a brain. They are going to have to ask why it is that we can only accept that something is scientific if it displays the three predominant characteristics of the natural sciences, which is that they must display predictability, repeatability and mathematical quantifiability.

That, by definition, precludes intuition, subjective judgement, tacit knowledge, heuristics, dreams, imagination and all those things which make us precious as human beings.

1992 will occur at the beginning of the 1990s. I hold that, properly handled, this provides us all with a great opportunity. Europe has an economic base big enough, an internal market strong enough, a culture rich and diverse enough, to allow us to develop forms of science and technology, educational forms and social structures which would accord with our cultural, geographical and other realities.

But unless we have people, young and old, who understand that possibility and are willing to stand up and fight for it, the reverse could be the case. There is already talk in the EC about the danger of a periphery. By that, they mean that the polarisation of activity which in the past meant that people were driven to London, Birmingham, Newcastle and Manchester to seek work in the United Kingdom will now be repeated at the macro level in the EC. The 'periphery' is viewed by these people as being all of Denmark, Germany down as far as Essen, the north of England, all of Ireland, all of Greece, all of Portugal and southern Italy. It is precisely on this periphery that the richest cultures in Ireland and in Europe still exist – the Celtic culture, the Scandinavian and the Greek cultures.

It is going to require people to understand these dangers and also understand the opportunities. Ricardo Patrella of FAST in Brussels predicts that, if we don't act now, a hundred thousand small towns will cease to exist, with all that that implies for us. I guess they will become holiday homes.

We already have 16 million people out of work in the EC and even if we could maintain the present growth rates, there will be something like 20 million people out of work by 1994.

Our educational system is going to have to produce people who can face that kind of challenge – those who are self-starters, who have the imagination to get up and do things and to provide a framework in which Ireland will be able to deal with its situation: a country with a mere 4 million people and yet with one of the highest exports of its talent all over Europe.

The 21st century should not be viewed as an extrapolation from the past. We should have the courage to look idealistically at where we would like to be and then look backwards to see what the impediments are which will prevent us getting there. When I say 'we should look idealistically', it suddenly occurs to me that to talk about people as idealists nowadays is a term of abuse, which shows the stage to which our society has degenerated. In the Renaissance, such people would have been cherished. There will be great danger from 1992 that Europe will become a melting pot, as the United States did at the turn of the last century. There is a real danger that the cultural imperialism of the English language will destroy a vast range of highly important, colourful and descriptive languages in Europe. Even the German language, rooted as it is in the most powerful economy in Western Europe, now doesn't have a word for 'software' or 'hardware'. It doesn't mean that they've accepted two foreign words. They've accepted a whole ideological assumption through this awful 'Tayloristic'

Americanised way of viewing technology which says that, on the one hand, there is software and, on the other hand, hardware – quite contrary to the whole German Hegelian way of viewing things as being a totality.

Europe's strength is its diversity and we are moving into an era in which we will be moving from economy of scale to economy of scope as environmental and other matters bear in on top of us. Ireland and Irish culture could make an incredible contribution to that development. Precisely at a time when our thinking is being dominated by narrow rationalist quantification, our Irish culture with its linguistic richness, its linguistic forms, its sense of drama, its sense of descriptiveness could have a significant impact – it would be tragic if that were to be lost. Of course, the pessimist will say, 'Well, it's all so small and so few people speak Irish, nothing can be done about it.'

There is no economic basis for saying that. In the Faroes, significantly smaller, with an even more marginalised language, there has been an incredible cultural renaissance, where the number of books produced – new books, pro rata – is higher than any place else in the world. New technology, properly used, means that we could even have one-off series of books. So that argument doesn't apply any longer.

Now, as we approach the 1990s, it seems to me that it is necessary courageously to re-examine what we mean by education. For me, it is a lifelong process, a state of mind. It is not just schools and universities. Indeed, in many ways I personally regard schools as a sort of historical aberration – we've only had them for two hundred years. I am not talking about the great schools of learning, as in Renaissance Florence, where people like Brunelleschi or Giotto or Leonardo would serve a seven-year apprenticeship, starting out as a goldsmith, and end up by building the greatest dome in Christendom, the cupola of Sancta Maria del Fiore. I am talking about arid forms of education and I guess, at a meeting like this, one should quote Ivan Illich:

> School is an institution built on the axiom that learning is the result of teaching, and this institutional wisdom continues to accept this axiom, in spite of overwhelming evidence to the contrary.

He goes on to say we have all known most of what we know outside school. Pupils do most of the learning without, and often despite, their teachers.

> Everyone learns how to live outside school, how to speak, how to think, how to love, how to feel, how to curse, how to politick and how to work without interference from a teacher.

Many teachers are highly talented, dedicated people. I was most fortunate in Tuam to meet a highly talented teacher of metalwork who inflamed my interest in engineering. But I talk here about that institution as a totality, which I think must come into question as we move into the 1990s.

Here of course in Ireland the school is a kind of *venturi* through which people are pressed in that frantic destructive sprint in which parents, teachers and universities conspire to pressurise people in an outrageous way towards the binary gate which switches from 'go' to 'no go' in the way that the most arid computer system might do. I know of no place else in Europe where young people are subjected to that kind of pressure. Only in Japan have I seen something parallel, and there they succeed in driving young people to suicide.

It is essential that we question all of this. I have never yet met a parent or teacher or university professor in this country who seems to approve it. They all 'tut-tut' to each other, but nobody seems to have the courage to do anything about it. It's essential that we begin to look at the varieties of ways of learning and developing that are already beginning to grow in other parts of Europe: alternative routes. In Germany, they firstly had the second route – they've now got the third route and the fourth route. These are routes by which one can qualify professionally by learning by doing and developing by doing. There is even a degree in medicine at McMaster University where you actually start out right from the beginning by working alongside an experienced practitioner and it produces some of the best medical practitioners that I know of in North America.

It is important that we have the courage to look at how we really learn. I was conscious in bringing up my own two sons with my wife (who is a teacher) that we both sought somehow to protect them from all those things which had really been the basis of everything we had learned. I was concerned that somehow my own logic was failing. If we look at the most profound thing we will ever learn in life, even if we ultimately take degrees in Theoretical Physics or doctorates in those subjects, the most profound thing is natural language. We learn natural language through the dynamic of doing it. In every language, there is some term like '*die Muttersprache*' – the mother tongue.

If a child were required to learn its first language like it is required to learn its second language, I do believe it would never learn to speak. If somebody said to it, 'This is a subordinate adjectival clause, a noun, a verb', it wouldn't even get going. Yet somehow we fail to accept the significance of that and distort every other form of educational development from that early stage.

My own view is that one hears and one forgets; one sees and one remembers; one does and one understands. We really do learn by doing. The important things I've learned – I don't wish to personalise things too much, but I do think of myself as an organic intellectual – I learned by doing. In Tuam as young children we used simply to play with pieces of wood and the game was to pass it round and see what we could envisage in that piece of wood. Some people would see skeletons, and other people would see dragons, and so on. I notice even today when I look at complex pages and pages of mathematical formulae, I somehow still have the capacity to see a pattern in that mass of things. A deep pattern recognition capability was developed at that early stage. We used to play with water in the Ballygaddy river and I remember making little locks and noticing how, as the water approached them, it increased in velocity – you put little ships on it and you could confirm this. I subsequently understood *venturi phenomena* and its related mathematics that much better precisely because I had gone through that kind of experience.

In Germany, some of the most experimental schools are found in the cities where young people are simply dropping out because they no longer accept what is on offer at the conventional schools. They have had the courage to take on board those kinds of experiences I have been talking about. So there are project-learning systems, where they perhaps adopt a river and the young children will produce small instruments in the physics class to measure its pollution; in the biology class they will take examples of its content; the children write beautiful poetry if they see dead fish floating on the river. That is real learning.

I think it's important as we approach the 1990s that we examine why it is that we degrade and demean that way of learning. The attitude to our technical schools, for example, is, in my view, appalling. I remember when I was in Tuam I was at the Christian Brothers and I did enjoy Latin and things like that as well. I really did. But I wanted to learn Technical Drawing and I determined I was going to go to the technical school to learn it, because it was not on offer at the Christian Brothers school.

Apparently, I was the first person in the town to enforce my own form of comprehensive education. But I remember Brother Rafferty, who was a very well-meaning if somewhat confused person, who didn't know the difference between qualitative and quantitative, telling me most seriously that I was going to destroy my educational career. Six months afterwards, Tom

Murphy followed me and was given the same dire warning. What he was saving Tom Murphy from was going through the Leaving Certificate, then probably going to do a degree in English, and ending up writing the same incredibly boring, but grammatically correct, English which the rest of us do. Instead he is, in my view, one of the Europe's most creative playwrights – because he went into the local sugar factory and was aware of all the tensions and subtle interactions in that environment.

Then in the west of Ireland there were women in the Claddagh still who used to weave shawls. I've seen people get degrees in Fine Art at the Royal College of Art in London who couldn't even begin to approach the skill and ability of those people. Yet that skill was transmitted organically from mother to daughter, as it was then.

Since the 15th century, we have deliberately downgraded that form of work which is manual and tactile. It started at the end of the Renaissance, when academics tried to prevent master builders using the term *magister* because it might have been confused with a Master of Arts from a university. When they found that in Alsace-Lorraine there was a tradition that, if you built twelve major structures with so many architectural elements, you'd be known as *Doctor Latimorum*, they actually tried to introduce laws to prevent this hideous development, namely, manual workers being called doctors. Yet it is precisely those manual workers who gave us the very basis of our western civilisation.

So intimidating was this embryonic arid academic approach that even people like Leonardo da Vinci (whom we now hold up as the pinnacle of our Renaissance person) had the following to say about these people:

> They will say that not having learning, I will not
> speak properly of that which I wish to elucidate,
> but do they not know that my subjects are the
> better illustrated from experience, than by yet

more words: experience, which has been the
mistress of all those who wrote well, and thus as
mistress, I will cite her in all cases.

The great Dürer, known to most people as an artist, was also
a great Professor of Mathematics. He actually pointed out
that it would be possible to develop new forms of mathematics,
which, as he put it, would be as amenable to the human spirit
as natural language. He was talking about a very different
form of learning and understanding.

We need forms which allow us to interact closely with nature
and learn from nature. I learned so much about aerodynamics
by watching trees in motion. My early insight into guidance
systems was when I wondered how the geese used to come to
the west of Ireland about this time each year – the third week
in October – and how they had guided themselves from Canada
and Siberia.

There was a sense in which one could see the greatness of
nature, and one began to understand that we had to accord
with it. I think people used to say *'Ní hé lá na gaoithe, lá na
scolb'*, which means that you actually mould what you're
doing, partly to accord with nature. It is most important as we
move towards the 1990s that we look at other cultures and
other ways of viewing these relationships. There's the great
saying from the North American Indian when his people were
being rounded up in the compound:

> I say to you my people, the paleface will take the
> eagle from the sky, he will take the salmon from
> the streams, he'll take the buffalo from the plains,
> he'll poison the air that we breathe and the water
> that we drink.

That was much more accurate a prediction than the Hudson
Institute of Futurology was able to do even ten years ago,
because he saw precisely what it was we were doing to nature
and to ourselves. I can't imagine that if one had that relationship
and concern with nature one could contemplate, as apparently

is now the case, that fertiliser will be poured on the Burren in the west of Ireland.

It is going to be essential in the 1990s to develop forms of education which do not confuse linguistic ability with intelligence. I'm not here talking about the capacity to tell stories or be descriptive – I hold that to be a marvellous attribute. I'm talking about that narrow point of view, the belief that unless you can write a great thesis about something, you don't actually understand it. Most people I know express their intelligence by what they do and how they do it, rather than the way they write and talk about it. I saw at Lucas Aerospace the incredible creativity and energy of people if a framework was set up which allowed them to use their talents in that sort of way.

It is going to be essential that we end the division between young and old people. It is already predicted, in Britain in any case, that 80 percent of all those who will be working in commerce and industry in the next century are already there. There are terrific demographic shifts taking place which will require educational forms that allow people to continue to develop right through their lives; that you don't just switch off at fifty.

In that sense, I think the Greeks had it absolutely correct when they used to suggest, 'how dull it is to pause, to make an end, to rust unburnished, not to shine in use'. There is a wealth of talent around amongst people that could be marshalled to deal with the problems of our society; vast packages of knowledge, which could be handed on to future generations.

It is going to be essential in the '90s in the field of science and technology that we create environments in which more women will come into science and technology – not as imitation men or as honorary males or grotesque Margaret Thatcher-like figures – but with the courage to question the male value system, which, in my view, has dominated western science and technology for too long.

We should create joint courses where people can study both Science and Arts together. I worked for a long time on a very interesting computer system which works out a transformation from data to information, from information to knowledge, knowledge to wisdom, wisdom to action. It is a kind of cybernetic loop which is now being researched at the University of Tokyo. I was quite proud about this little invention of mine until one of my colleagues said, 'I'm sure I saw something like that in a poem from TS Eliot.' And sure enough I got out the *Collected Works* and there was a poem which concluded by saying:

> What wisdom have we lost in knowledge
> What knowledge have we lost in information.

So often artists and writers and poets will prefigure the big issues in society, and we do ourselves great damage as engineers and scientists if we separate ourselves from that.

Above all else, it is going to be necessary to kindle a sense of imagination and excitement. When you say that, people will say, 'Well, that may be all right in music or in literature', but you look at what the great scientists have to say. The great Einstein said, 'Imagination is far more important than knowledge.' And he went on to say:

> The mere formulation of a problem is far more important than its solution, which might be merely a matter of experimental or mathematical skill. To raise new problems, to look at old problems from a new aspect marks the real advances in science.

When he was being pressed by one of these arid reductionists at the MIT to say how it was that he arrived at the Theory of Relativity, they would have loved if he agreed that it was some narrow mathematical regression, where you squeezed out the only answer in a regression which led you to the one best way. Einstein horrified them, apparently, by suddenly saying, 'When I was a child of fourteen I asked myself what it might be like to ride on a beam of light and look back at the world.' A beautiful conceptual framework to which he subsequently provided the mathematics.

It is going to require a lot of courage to face up to these issues because we have been so dominated by this reductionist type of thinking, that it will require great personal courage and people perhaps sacrificing their careers to question these issues. Nations as a whole will have to show their courage. I find it extraordinary that a nation which had the courage to stand up for eight hundred years to an apparently implacable enemy – British Imperialism – at a time when there was hardly a crack in its edifice, and was able, generation after generation, to produce people who asserted the right to nationhood and to its culture, now seems to be so disoriented and so apathetic about the situation which faces it.

Above all else, it seems to me, it is going to be necessary to look at the skills and interests of people, to build on the positive things about human beings. There is an awful characteristic, which is common also in Ireland, to look at people's weaknesses. The very basis of our examinations is to find out what people *don't* know, rather than what they *do* know. People laugh when they hear of the tradition that used to be at Cambridge which is: if you got a question you didn't like, you just ignored it and wrote your own question. That really is what life is about – writing your own questions and answering them in a profound way. That's what people do when they do an MA or a PhD. I think this terrible emphasis on what people don't know, this destructiveness, putting people down, was most powerfully expressed by James Joyce in *Finnegans Wake*, where he described the two characters in any human being, Shem and Shaun, and he warned us of the danger of concentrating on the negative character:

> Sniffer of carrion, premature gravedigger, seeker
> of the nest of evil in the bosom of good word,
> you who sleep at our vigil and fast at our feast,

you with your dislocated reason, you've reared
your disunited kingdom on the vacuum of your
own most intensely doubtful soul.

I think we have to transcend our 'doubtful souls' and be willing
to question some of these issues I have described.

Ann Higgins

I propose to explore and examine the concept of Irish education and what that means for the 1990s. First, I will give a little information about my background to set my thoughts and my ideals in context.

Myself

In 1980 I qualified as a primary school teacher and for five years did a combination of classroom teaching and remedial work. Then for the past four years, I have worked in Killeely Community Project in Limerick, working with a community, struggling with the adults and child to identify their various needs and to try to meet them. The project began by parents of the children of the school coming together one morning per week for a number of months to learn ways in which they themselves could become the teachers of their children. They were learning about how a child learns, how a child can be helped within the home. The project grew, the adults went on to identify their own specific needs and so a grassroots community project was born. Over the four years we have run a very large variety of adult classes. Some of the teachers were drawn from within the community itself, women who were willing to share their skills and talents with their neighbours. Other teachers have been provided through Limerick City VEC, whose Adult Education Officer, Deirdre Frawley, is very committed to bringing educational and learning opportunities into the community.

There is also a supplementary school, called The Three O'Clock School, as part of that project. It operates after official school hours and it offers a variety of learning opportunities to children, but more important than that, it offers children and adults the opportunity to be involved in a learning situation together. The Three O'Clock School at present has 20 children, 3 mothers, one voluntary worker and myself. It operates four days per week, providing social, creative and remedial learning opportunities for children and adults. It works with family groups – so the age range of the children in the group is from one year to 14 years. I have also done some voluntary literacy work with 16-year-old youngsters who have dropped out of the school system at an early age.

Learning

Education is a funny word – it evokes different responses from different people. For some, education has meant the road to success; for others, it leaves a bad taste in their mouths – a sense of failure and a sense of hurt. But let us leave that aside for a little while – let us divorce ourselves from our personal experiences and look at education in a clear light. I would like to free myself further and use the word 'learning' instead of 'education'.

For me, learning is a lifelong phenomenon – watching a three-month-old baby learning about her hands or an old man learning to use a walking aid – these are very valid learning experiences; obviously, we learn different things at different stages of our lives. I believe that learning should be holistic, it should be exciting, it should be appropriate to the individual's needs at that time of their lives. I believe that the learning opportunities we provide our children with should enable them to become confident, responsible, happy people, able to participate in and to enrich the community in which they live. There is a definite link between the learning opportunities on offer to a child or to an adult and the quality of that person's life. I would also hope that they would become confident in themselves as individual people.

For me, learning is the spark of life – whether it means the discovery of personal abilities and talents, or the discovery of the joys of nature. A learning situation which enriches a person has a spin-off effect into that person's family, into the community in which that person lives; to be a more holistic, happy person is to be an asset to the community in which that person lives. I believe there is a direct link between the education or the learning opportunities we offer and the type of society we live in. Our educational system is supported by the society, which is in turn supported by our educational system. So let's look at that educational system – let us look at what is on offer.

Primary Education Now

First of all, let us look at primary education. Basically we offer all children a place in a classroom along with thirty-eight others of the same age, plus an adult. That is what we offer him or her for the first eight or nine years of the educational journey. Is it fair to ask a child to sit in a desk with so big a crowd for so long? Is it fair to ask one adult to take responsibility for that number of children for 5½ hours per day? In fact, recently two speech therapists from the Mid-Western Health Board went to Mary Immaculate College to talk to the students because so many teachers were going to them with voice troubles – the problem with teachers' voices was because of the large numbers in the classroom, because of the strain placed on a teacher working in that situation. Can the needs of the slow learner, the emotionally disturbed, or the very bright child be met in that environment?

What has happened is that we have given our children into a system where one adult is entrusted with their education for a year at a time. Parents and other members of the community do not normally interact with this process, except to help with homework. One bright six-year-old I know spends two hours per evening doing his homework – where is his time for play, where is his time for his family? Why can't more adults be involved in a looser system? Why have parents become disassociated from the education of their children?

What happens to the child who finishes his or her participation in the system when he or she leaves primary school – maybe often going on to do a six-month or a nine-month course, maybe moving from one course to another, or maybe just dropping out? Is it fair to expect the teacher to organise learning opportunities which are individually appropriate for all thirty-nine children? Is the classroom the only place the child of primary school age can be involved in learning? What about the other areas of the community – the church, the community hall, the fields, the woods, the lakes, the streets – what does a child of that age need to learn? What about the talents and skills of other adults in the community – the storyteller, the gardener, the shopkeeper, the housekeeper, the craftsperson, the cleaning person, the priest, the guard, the farmer, the fisherman – how can they be involved in the education of the children? How can they share their skills and pass on their knowledge? Is the model of thirty-nine children to one adult the best we can offer our children? They are entitled to their heritage – to inherit the knowledge that has been accumulated by their forebears – how can we give them their inheritance with the knowledge that the future of our society is ultimately dependent on our youth? We do not simply inherit the earth from our parents – we guard it for our children.

Let us not allow ourselves to be locked within a system. Why not explore other areas, other ways? I'm not an educational historian, but I believe this rigid classroom model is quite young – yet we seem to have accepted it as if it were sacred and unchangeable. Let's focus on a four- or five-year-old child going to school. Yes, I know many of them are happy – many adults say that the children going to school nowadays are much happier than they themselves were – but let's not be satisfied with that alone. I believe that a child needs to develop his or her talents and abilities. Apart from the academic side, the child needs to express himself or herself through crafts and through sports – needs to interact not only with the home and school, but also with the wider environment. A child needs to develop his or her ability to question, to see things from different angles, to be tolerant of differences in people, but, most of all, a child needs to dream, to explore and to enjoy being a child.

I was talking to a neighbour recently, an older woman. She was telling me that a neighbour visited her mother the other day and she said, 'The children aren't home from school yet,' and her mother said, 'Ah, they have a while yet, they're grazing home from school.' The amount that they were learning on the way home was very great – and I just wish that every child had that opportunity.

Where is the spark of the individual? A child wears a uniform like all the other children in the school and carries a schoolbag laden down with books produced by publishers who have no knowledge of the life of that child.

Post-Primary Education Now

What is on offer at second level? There's a points system that discourages co-operation; a rat-race to see who the succeeders are and we award the succeeders by allowing them to go on to third level if they can afford it, to further run the gauntlet and maybe then what? Emigrate? Is that success? Is our educational system creating and upholding a society in which the most important value is the survival of the fittest? I recently encountered, in a book called *The One Straw Revolution,* the following:

> Formal schooling has no intrinsic value but becomes necessary when humanity creates a condition in which one needs to become educated to get along.

The technically and academically bright have been awarded money and status by society, by the educational system – yet the person who cares for the old, for the children, for the neighbour, for the land and for the sea has not been awarded such status. The educational system by its structures, by the way it awards merits to the academic achievers, creates the failures and decides what it is that our society should hold in esteem. It awards payments for different tasks carried out.

Yet it is often these academically brilliant people – not all of them, some of them – who have created nuclear power, who explode bombs under the desert, who test their devices to the genetic peril of less powerful cultures. It is also the succeeders who make high level decisions, decisions to store mountains of food, while millions of people die of hunger. Does the race for points help the teenager to be more a responsible enriched member of society? The education provided by a society reflects the philosophy of that society to a great degree. Therefore, when we examine the educational system, we are also looking at the society in which that system is in operation.

I don't think it is possible to suggest changes within an educational system without realising that this means changes within the society. I would like to see a society based on sharing and justice. I would like to see hierarchical power structures, whether they be church or state, replaced by structures where people at grassroots have more input into the decision-making process.

The clearest example of this phenomenon of second level education I encountered recently on an *Open Mind* programme. It was a programme where a group of boys from a secondary boarding school were interviewed. They were away from their families and communities; the rules within that very school kept them away from the society in which that building was located. They couldn't actually go down town, couldn't smoke, they had no opportunity to meet girls. Their day was organised like clockwork, free time was from 10 until 10.30 in the evening when there was a long queue for the phones, to phone home. I think that speaks for itself. How were these young men to learn how to relate to young women? How to relate to children? How to relate to the old? How to relate to a new-born baby? How to relate to the sick? Have we placed educational achievement so high on our list of priorities that we allow our young people to be imprisoned away from life in order to attain the desired academic standard, to satisfy the requirements of a third level institution by increasing their points requirements every year? And does the choice of courses taken at third level reflect the personal interests and talents of the individual or does it represent the ever-changing demands of the employment market?

Adult Education

And what do we offer adults by way of education? We offer them one-sixth of one percent of the total education budget. It is a fact that over the years the people who have benefited most from adult education classes have been those who are furthering their education; those who have already 'benefited', if that is the word, from the system. Adult education benefits adults and has a trickle-down effect into the family. Adult education must become more available to all, not just to the people who have money to pay for a set of ten classes, but to the people who are less well off. Adults must be facilitated to take an active part in their own learning – crèches, etc. must be provided. Adult education doesn't simply mean classes in carpentry or cookery – it may mean classes in confidence-building, in assertiveness training, in coping with stress; it means classes or groups for whatever the needs are that those adults themselves identify.

I am proud to say that adult education opportunities in Limerick are being made more and more accessible to people living within less well-off communities. Many people who might have left the educational system early and now want to be part of a learning process have the opportunity to do so. This is due greatly to the personal efforts of Deirdre Frawley, the Adult Education Officer with Limerick City VEC, who encourages community development and was also involved in piloting the EOS – the Educational Opportunities Scheme, which allowed adults to study for the Leaving Certificate while drawing the dole.

Inequality

A very serious facet of our educational system is the inequalities within it. In a country that purports to cherish all her children equally, parents of poorer children struggle to provide books and uniforms and all other costs that arise weekly for the school-going child. Education costs the poorer family a lot of money. Being poor also means that the cost of second level education puts great stress on the family budget. Several studies have shown that the percentage of children from working-class backgrounds in third level education is minimal compared with wealthier people in our society.

We live in a society in which the child of the rich and the child of the poor have very different prospects. For me, equality means providing each and every child with the best possible opportunities for learning and enrichment. The only sane investment we can make for the future of our society is an investment in our children. Let us invest our time and our resources so they can be responsible, whole people able to interact and improve our society and environment.

A Saner Alternative

True, I have highlighted much of what is wrong. I am not criticising individuals or pointing a finger. I am encouraging all who are involved in education to be adventurous. So what alternatives would I propose? What other ways could we organise our learning? I have no cut and dried answers, but I do have insights which might act as building blocks to a more sane alternative. I think a lot of valuable energy could be lost in pointing fingers and in blaming different people for the obvious gaps in our educational system. I would much prefer to see a pooling of energies of all involved in education in an effort to arrive at an alternative more in keeping with the principles and guidelines which would afford us a saner and more humane educational system and society.

I would like to propose some practical steps in breaking down barriers which have been erected and in forging more honest and direct communication between those involved in the process of education and learning. I would like to see a lot more teacher/parent interaction in a positive way. Teachers often say it is hard to get the parents into the school and I would say that a lot of the time when the parents are invited into the school, it is to hear complaints that such-and-such a child has been bold, or to get money or books or whatever. There must be *real* involvement. Therefore, that means assessing the role and function of the physical school building in the community. Is it just a building used from 9 to 3 by X number of adults and Y number of children? Or can we look at that school building as a resource for the community? Many schools have halls, stages with lighting, blackboards, tape recorders, projectors, laboratories, computers, musical instruments, libraries, etc. So if we talk of using the school building in a different way, there are obvious problems arising. Who will lock and open the doors? Who will be responsible for the equipment? Who will turn on and off the heating? These are the things that cause a lot of stress. Who will take bookings for the use of the rooms? Who will take the responsibility? There's obviously a full-time job as caretaker/administrator there. And maybe this is an opportune time because, with declining family numbers, many schools now have empty rooms and maybe we could look at different ways of using them.

What about involving parents and adults more in a classroom situation? I know in England, apart from having a teacher in a classroom, there is a job as a teacher's aide, where another adult, who is not a trained teacher, is in the classroom with the teacher, and helps with painting and storytelling and tying shoelaces and gets involved in a very real way in the learning process of the child.

I would also see the need for a professional child-care worker to be attached to the school. In my day, which is nearly ten years ago, teacher training was very much to do with methodology of teaching; maybe the whole idea of 'teacher' can be reviewed. I would like to see a teacher as a resource person, an enabler, as a facilitator of learning, being open-minded about what that might involve. A teacher needs to know the community in which he or she is operating, needs to be aware of how unemployment affects people, of how illness in the family affects the child, of how family strife might affect the child. So I am talking about a re-orientation of the role of teacher with the help of a child-care worker, with the continued involvement of parents and of people in the community. I would propose breaking down barriers – as a first step by people calling each other by their names. I think it is dreadful for a parent to go up to a classroom to say Miss this, or Mr that.

I have spoken about people coming into the school and being involved, about the school building becoming a learning centre, a hive of activity. What of changing the concept of learning just taking place in a school? A lot can be learned by visiting a farm, from contact with the soil, with growing things, with animals; a child can learn respect for life, maybe visiting a factory to see how things are made, maybe visiting and spending time in a craft workshop – the possibility of young children being involved in different learning situations – many children never see where their parents may be working outside of the home.

I think it must be quite exciting to teach your own child at home – and parents who choose to do so should receive whatever support and backup they feel they need. I think the personal talents of the teacher, of the child, or the parents are the bonus in the learning situation and that these talents need to be shared to the greatest level possible. I believe learning is very important and rather more than simply imparting knowledge.

A major development I would like to see is to develop and to encourage in the child and adult the ability to question. It is innate in a child, as any parent of a two- or three-year-old who spends their days answering, 'What is this?' and 'What is that?' will tell you. Yet, in a classroom where there are thirty-nine children, it is not possible continually to answer individual questions and get involved. We all have the right to ask questions – not just to accept somebody else's interpretation of life. We need to develop the skills to use a library, to use videos, skills to go down and ask the 90-year-old man or woman what it was like for them when they were a child. Parents and other adults in the community have a heritage and skills to pass on. Somehow parents have got around to thinking what they have to offer is not as important as the points in the Leaving Certificate.

Being Irish

I have spoken at length about the meaning of education, about the implications our understanding of it has for our society. But what about what it means to be Irish? How can we organise our educational system so that it reflects what it means to be Irish? With the onslaught of 1992, with television blasting American and Australian and other cultures at us, it is very important to hang on to and to cherish our Irishness. We are a small island at the edge of Europe. Let us be a society with vision. Let us not turn our backs on our heritage of music, of song, of stories, of learning, of craft skills.

Let us not turn our backs on all it means to be Irish. Let us not trade that with some other cultures without realising the loss, and at the same time let us open our minds to what is coming in.

We must build into our society learning opportunities where children will learn the value of being Irish. We must tell our youth that it is good to be Irish and we must demonstrate this by providing and encouraging a society based more on equality, based more on honest relationships between people. I think that the basis of learning is about relationships – the relationship between the child and adult, between adults and adults, between men and women, young and old, child and child. It is about the relationship between ourselves and our environment; between ourselves and our history – or 'herstory' – and between ourselves and the heritage that we have.

Dedication

My last comment is that the most learned and the most wise people I have met in my life are the people the system would not deem a success. I dedicate this talk to the women and children of Killeely who have taught me more about life and love than any system anywhere could ever teach. Thank you, Clare Flynn, principal of St Lelia's National School, Killeely for your encouragement and motivation; thank you, Deirdre Frawley, Adult Education Officer, Limerick City VEC, for your commitment to bring learning opportunities into the community, for your support, not alone of the projects that I'm involved in, but of the many others throughout the city. Thank you to all the women and children whom I have had the privilege to accompany on an educational journey.

1990

HEALTH, WEALTH AND WISDOM FOR THE 21ST CENTURY

SPEAKER

James Robertson

Former policy-maker with the British government and for the past twenty-five years an independent writer and thinker, arguing strongly for a saner, more humane and more enabling worldview

James Robertson

For most business people, bureaucrats and politicians in the countries of Western Europe like yours and mine, 1992 means the European Single Market. I hesitate to call this a short-sighted and narrow view, taken by those who cannot see further than the end of their nose or – as the Indian saying has it – wider than the tips of their ears.

But the historical significance of 1992 is much more far-reaching, much less parochial, than the European Single Market.

In 1992, for the first time in history, representatives of all the peoples of the world will come together to discuss our common future – at the United Nations Conference on Environment and Development in Brazil. This will be held on the 20th anniversary of the 1972 Stockholm Conference on the environment. It will be the first major landmark in the follow-up to the Brundtland Commission's report *Our Common Future*, published in 1987.

And, more significant still, 1992 will be the 500th anniversary of Columbus' landing in the Western hemisphere.

Many people of European, or Western, outlook will celebrate Columbus' achievement as the 'discovery' of America – as if the indigenous peoples of the continent did not exist and were of no account. From that Eurocentric point of view, October 12th 1492 was an unqualified 'good thing' – in Sellars' and Yeatman's phrase from *1066 and All That* – a historic milestone in the upward progress of the human race from savagery to civilisation.

To the indigenous peoples of North and South America, it is a different story. They will have little to celebrate in 1992. To them, Columbus was a historic disaster – leading to the loss of their traditional freedoms and livelihoods, the devastation of their lands, and the destruction of their cultures. That story continues today, for those like the Yanomani and other forest peoples of the Amazon basin.

And not only for them. The same is true for other non-European peoples all over the planet. For them, Columbus in 1492, and Vasco da Gama sailing to India in 1498, signify the beginning of half a millennium of European world domination – at first Christian and latterly secular.

I don't want to deny that this 500-year epoch has brought progress of many kinds – though this raises questions about how we define progress. A generation or two ago, it might have made sense to interpret the competitive success of European, or Western, culture simply as an example of Darwinism – the survival of the fittest. But, as things are now turning out, that might seem like a sick joke. For it is the kinds of progress European culture has brought to the world, and the direction of further development it entails, that are now the gravest threat to human survival.

Weapons development is one obvious aspect of this.

More deeply dangerous, because a little less obvious, is the vision of the good life – the high consumption lifestyle – which we relentlessly promote worldwide as the main goal of development. I'm not just thinking of African villagers watching *Dallas* on TV, though that is an example.

With the 5 billion people now in the world, we are already threatening the Earth's life support systems. Projections show that the number will ultimately rise to 10 or 15 billion. If development, as we now promote it, were fully successful and all these 10 or 15 billion people were to consume as many resources and cause as much pollution as today's rich minority (which includes you and me), today's ecological impacts would be multiplied by 20 or 30 times. Anyone who thinks this makes sense must be crazy. I said that the dangers might not be immediately obvious. But, in fact, even some mainstream economists are now beginning to put out blueprints for a greener economy.

We urgently need to switch to a new development path. We need a new way of economic life and thought. It must be enabling for people, not disabling and dependency-creating, as much economic progress is today. And it must be conserving for the Earth, not ecologically damaging and destructive.

This switch to a new economics must be part of a larger 'paradigm shift'. Conventional economics is part of our prevailing worldview. That worldview – and the existing world order based on it – are beginning to break down. One of the main tasks, the historic role, you might say, for us who are living at this time, is to help to bring into being a new worldview and a new world order.

This has tremendous implications, and there are very many aspects we could explore. What I want to do in this talk is to look at the need for a new economics in the context of that larger paradigm shift – that is to say, in the context of the history and the future of ideas.

The European Inheritance

The addictive, destructive and unsustainable approach to economic life which now prevails in almost every corner of the world is linked to the dominance of European culture and the Western worldview.

So where did we Europeans go wrong? Where did our European inheritance play us false?

One view is that the damage was done when the medieval order in Europe broke down. Although we can't go back to the Middle Ages, looking at what happened then may help us to see our way forward now.

The medieval worldview was hierarchical, static, religious and moral.

The medieval hierarchy started with God in his Heaven at the top, followed by archangels and angels. Then came humankind, below the angels but above the beasts. Highest among humans were popes and kings, followed by princes and bishops and nobles, and so on down the line to the poorest of the common people. Then came the animal kingdom, with the vegetable and mineral orders of creation following on below.

The medieval picture of the world was static. Evolution played no part in it. People were expected to remain in the station in which God had placed them in society – the rich man in his castle and the poor man at his gate. Sons would follow in their fathers' footsteps. The village baker's son would become the village baker after him, the miller's son the miller, and so on. There was not much scope for yuppies in the Middle Ages. Upward mobility – and downward mobility, for that matter – were exceptions to the rule.

Above all, the medieval worldview was religious and moral. The central purpose of human life – the purpose that gave it meaning – was to save one's soul for eternal life with God and his angels in another world from this one. The workings of God's creation, including the behaviour of human beings, were governed by God's laws. Economic transactions and relationships were subject to moral law: the just price and the just wage were part of the divinely sanctioned web of rights and obligations that held everyone and everything together.

That hierarchical, static, religious and moral worldview, which had been dominant in the Middle Ages, broke down about 500 years ago, as did the structures of society and ways of life based on it. It broke down because the old order had become unsustainable, and because the way to a new future was being opened up by pioneers like Columbus and Machiavelli (1469-1527) and Copernicus (1473-1543), breaking through previous limitations of territory, behaviour and thought.

Much the same dynamic – breakdown of the old and breakthrough to the new – is at work today. The worldview now dominant, and the structures of society and the ways of life based on it, are becoming unsustainable. And pioneers in many fields – including the growing worldwide movement for a new economics – are opening up the way to a new future, whose characteristic worldview, structures of society and ways of life we still have to crystallise.

Origins of the Modern Worldview

When the medieval worldview broke down, it took some time – nearly 300 years – for the modern worldview to crystallise in its place. This time, the process will have to be quicker. Nonetheless, what happened then is interesting and relevant for us today.

Among the thinkers who helped to shape the modern worldview were Descartes, Francis Bacon, Newton and Hobbes. Theirs were among the ideas that Adam Smith took up when, in the Enlightenment of the 18th century, he systematised the modern approach to economic life and thought.

Descartes divided reality into two categories, *res cogitans* and *res extensa* (thinking matter and extended matter). In due course, knowledge and science concentrated on, and came to regard as real, only the second part of that Cartesian duality – that is, those aspects of human experience and understanding which are material and measurable and outside ourselves. And Descartes' analytical method encouraged us to split those aspects of reality up into separate fields. So that now, for example, our conventional way of understanding what we take to be health, wealth and wisdom is splintered among different professional disciplines called medicine, economics and philosophy.

Bacon encouraged knowledge and science to focus on harnessing and exploiting the resources of Nature – Nature corresponding more or less to Descartes' *res extensa*. Bacon taught us to torture Nature in order to learn her secrets, and to use her for, as he put it, 'the relief of the inconveniences of man's estate'. So that now we are beginning to inflict catastrophic damage on the natural world.

Newton's example led science to interpret reality in the form of mechanistic, mathematically structured, value-free systems. So scientists now teach us to understand the workings of the universe in terms of numbers, and to assume that neither it nor any of its component parts are guided by purposes or moral choices.

What most people probably remember about Hobbes is his argument that, since, in fact – regardless of what theory might say – moral or divine law does not effectively control people's behaviour, they must submit to control by an earthly sovereign. Otherwise their lives are bound to be 'poor, solitary, nasty, brutish and short'. Hobbes' significance for us is that, like Machiavelli before him, he taught his successors to see human society, not as it ought to be, but as it actually appeared to be – a competitive struggle for power. So that very many people now take it for granted that success in life means getting one up on other people – or at least keeping up with the Joneses.

It was on ideas such as these, then, that Adam Smith drew in systematising his – and our – understanding of economic life. They are all ideas that we now need to question.

For example, Smith followed Descartes in excluding from economic understanding the less tangible aspects of human experience and activity, such as those we now call 'participation', 'self-fulfilment' and 'self-development'. He followed Bacon in accepting that economic life was about exploiting the resources of Nature for human advancement. He followed Hobbes in interpreting economic life as a competitive struggle for power – in particular, power over the use and the products of other people's labour. He followed Newton in seeing economic life as a value-free system, governed by its own impersonal laws. Smith's 'invisible hand' of supply and demand meant that God no longer had a part to play in economic life. It made God redundant – put Him out of a job. And Smith excluded not just religion, but morality too. He taught that the economic system operates best in the interest of all, if each pursues his own self-interest. As he put it,

> It is not from the benevolence of the butcher, the brewer or the baker that we expect our dinner, but from their regard to their own interest.

Another important point that Smith took for granted was that economic life revolves around money – prices, wages, profits, rents, and so forth. Now, money means numbers. And there's a very significant parallel between the emphasis on numerical data in modern science and the emphasis on money values in modern economic life.

The supremacy of quantitative values in modern scientific knowledge was nicely put by a scientist called Lord Kelvin. He said,

> When you can measure what you are speaking of and express it in numbers, you know that on which you are discoursing, but when you cannot measure it and express it in numbers, your knowledge is of a very meagre and unsatisfactory kind.

As with knowledge, so with value. Money puts numbers on value, and conventional economic understanding regards as very meagre and unsatisfactory the value of goods, services, and work (such as what used to be called women's work) which are not paid for with money. In fact, so far as economists are concerned, if you can't count something, it doesn't count. They just don't notice it. They blank it out.

This has led some critics – half-humorously – to interpret economics as a form of brain damage. Others, in similar vein, think economists are suffering from a lack of investment in up-to-date capital equipment. But I mustn't start telling jokes about economists or we will be here all night. The serious point is that there is an aspect of reality here which we are going to have to rethink in the post-modern world.

We are going to have to learn to value other forms of knowledge – personal, intuitive, moral and spiritual – as well as the knowledge offered by conventional science. We are going to have to learn to value what are called alternative or complementary approaches to health, as well as conventional medicine. We are going to have to learn to value informal economic activities – everything people do for themselves and one another without either paying or being paid – as well as activities whose value can be measured in money.

It will not be easy to marry the qualitative and the quantitative. They often conflict. For example, scientifically controlled monitoring of mystical experiences may destroy the conditions in which mystical experiences take place – like looking for darkness with a torch. But we are going to have to find ways to systematise new understandings – new theories – about knowledge, health and wealth which give full weight to both qualitative and quantitative values. Perhaps future historians of thought will see these new understandings and theories as post-scientific and post-medical and post-economic.

Recovery of Purpose

So let us now compare the modern worldview with the medieval worldview.

The modern worldview has remained hierarchical; it continues to see the world in terms of ladders. But it is mobile, not static. It sees human progress in terms of climbing a ladder of knowledge and power. It sees human life as a competition to climb higher than other people up ladders of career and status and wealth and power. And, when it can, it judges progress in terms of numerical measurements.

But, most importantly, the modern worldview has excluded religion and morality. It has offered no meaning to human life,

no goal at the top of the ladders, no purpose in climbing the
ladders other than climbing for its own sake. 'Ladders to
Nowhere' – that is the name of the game the modern worldview
asks us to play.

Even the most advanced scientists still suspect the very idea
of purpose, and assume that what they call 'objectivity'
excludes it. In his recent book *The Ages of Gaia*, James
Lovelock endorses the view that,

> … the cornerstone of scientific method is the
> postulate that Nature is objective. True knowledge
> can never be gained by attributing 'purpose' to
> phenomena.

That's what Lovelock says, and many people have hailed his
Gaia theory as a new milestone in science. But can you really
understand people without attributing purposes to them? Or
cats? Or earthworms? Or plants? Or the component parts of
any organism? And who is to say – how could anyone know?
– that true knowledge can be gained of the Universe itself by
assuming in advance that it has no purpose?

These are difficult questions. But one thing is absolutely
clear. The theoretical notion that scientific knowledge and
economic behaviour are value-free has left a vacuum. And in
practice this vacuum has been filled by values of power and
greed and competition.

In short, our European worldview has led us – and now the
rest of the world – to err and stray from the ways of wisdom.
There is now no health in us, in the old senses of wholeness
and holiness. And the kind of wealth we strive for is often not
wealth in the old sense of wellbeing – whether the wellbeing
of other people, or of the Earth, or even of ourselves. The
world's crisis today is a crisis of values.

Revival of Ethical Values

We have seen that the breakdown of the medieval worldview
meant the decline of an existing moral order and the rise of a

new scientific order. By contrast, I see the breakdown of the modern worldview as the decline of the existing scientific order and the rise of a new moral order. This will be clearer to future historians than it is to us now, but the signs are already there.

Take economics. The existing science of economics has told us that the chief aim of economic life is to make money values grow. So a national economy's chief aim has been money-measured economic growth, a business's chief aim has been financial profit, and the chief aim of consumers and investors has been to get best value for money from their purchases and the best financial return from their investments.

But in the 1980s these assumptions have begun to be questioned – even in the most respectable quarters.

For example, the World Bank and the International Monetary Fund are now beginning to recognise the devastating consequences of conventional economic orthodoxy for many Third World countries, and are beginning to face up to the need to resolve the long-running Third World debt crisis. Meanwhile, many people all round the world are not just feeling that the systematic transfer of wealth from poorer and less powerful peoples to richer and more powerful ones is wrong – which it clearly is. They are also recognising it as an inevitable outcome of a competitive, amoral economic system, driven by the aim of making money values grow, and regulated by the impersonal mechanics of supply and demand.

Another example is from the Brundtland Commission's report, *Our Common Future*. Brundtland pointed out that environmental policy and economic policy must be integrated. It is no longer good enough for environmental policy just to clear up the messes left by economic development, and to deal with what Brundtland called,

> ... after-the-fact repair of damage; reforestation, reclaiming desert lands, rebuilding urban environments, restoring natural habitats, and rehabilitating wild lands.

And it is no longer good enough for economic policy just to 'create wealth' in the narrow and abstract conventional sense, regardless of the environment.

In almost exactly the same way, the World Health Organisation (WHO), with its strategy on Health for All by the year 2000, has begun to shift the emphasis away from remedial sickness services to the positive creation of healthier conditions of life. WHO's conclusion on health, like Brundtland's on the environment, is that health goals must be brought into economic policy. Again, 'creating wealth' in the conventional sense is seen as too abstract and too narrow. Economic policy must pursue real purposes, like maintaining a good environment and enabling people to be healthy, and not just money-measured growth.

It is not just the conventional goals of economic policy that are beginning to be rethought, but also the conventional ways of measuring economic progress. A lot of work is getting under way – in the United Nations and national governments, as well as in activist groups like the New Economics Foundation – to develop and introduce new economic indicators and targets. This involves trying to improve existing money-measured indicators like Gross National Product (GNP). But, more importantly, it also involves supplementing these money-measured abstractions – perhaps eventually replacing them – by bringing into economic decision-making indicators of the state of the real world – which will show, for example, whether people's health, the cleanliness of air and water, and so on, are getting better or worse.

There is a parallel at the personal level to this bringing of real goals and purposes, and not just conventional money-measured criteria, into economic policy-making. I am talking about the increasing numbers of consumers and investors who are trying to be 'green', or 'ethical', or 'socially responsible'. They are deciding to bring their values into their economic lives, and to use their purchasing power and their investing power to support the kinds of projects and causes which they themselves favour. They are rejecting the conventional idea that their only economic goal should be to get best money value for themselves.

Even in science itself the idea of value-free objectivity is increasingly under fire. It is becoming more widely understood that, in many fields, objective knowledge is not even a theoretical possibility because the observer cannot observe the subject matter without affecting its behaviour in one way or another. In that respect, the particle physicist is in the same boat as the anthropologist studying a tribal society.

There is also growing awareness that the idea of value-free objectivity in science, just as in economics, has been used as a smokescreen by powerful groups – governments, business, finance, the military and the professions, including the scientific establishment itself – to use science in their own interests. In recent years, more and more people have become concerned about the purposes for which science is used.

Evolving a New Worldview

Those few examples of ethical purposes and moral choices being brought back into areas of practice and thought which the modern worldview has seen as value-free are pointers to the new worldview of the future. But what are they pointing us to? I can only give you my own personal thoughts.

Not back to the Middle Ages. Even if we could go back, the medieval picture of a static world is at odds with our knowledge of evolution today. The medieval assumption that the Christian God is superior to the divinities of other faiths does not fit the emerging multi-cultural one-world community of today. The medieval beliefs that God is masculine, that men are superior to women, and that humans are superior to Nature – special creatures with special kinds of souls to whom God has given dominion over the rest of His creation – clash with the feminist and ecological understandings of today.

Perhaps, then, in this coming post-European era of world history, we should turn to non-European faiths like Buddhism or Hinduism, or to the cultures of peoples like the Northern American Indians? They all offer wisdom about human life, and the place of human beings in the world, that has been lost in modern European culture. But, like Christianity, they have been quite unable to halt the worldwide juggernaut of conventional secular, consumerist development, although it runs contrary to their teachings. I am sure their insights will be reflected in the new worldview that eventually emerges. But, stemming as they did from small agricultural and pastoral and hunter-gatherer societies of long ago, we cannot realistically expect them to offer us a new post-modern worldview more or less ready-made, off the peg.

No. We should draw on the wisdom and insights of the past. But the peoples of the world today and tomorrow will have to create the new worldview afresh out of our own lives and predicaments, out of our own contemporary experience and understanding.

I think the new worldview will be a developmental worldview, in which purpose is combined with evolution in a new vision of progress. I think it will comprehend person and society, planet and universe, as aspects of the evolutionary process – a process which includes the evolution of consciousness and purpose – and perhaps of divinity too.

I think that what gives value and meaning to our lives will be the part we play in this process: developing our own potential, enabling other people to do the same, contributing to the development of our society and the emerging one-world human community, maintaining and perhaps even enhancing the natural riches of our planet, and consciously participating in the evolution of the cosmos.

That is the wider context in which the idea of a new, enabling and conserving economics makes sense to me. It is in that context, I foresee, that people in the next century and the next millennium will seek health, wealth and wisdom. It is in that context that we should interpret current issues – such as closer co-operation in Western Europe, or the collapse of communism in Eastern Europe, or the crisis in the Middle East. And it is in that context, I believe, that we should now be preparing to chart our common future in 1992.

Note

Fuller discussion of these questions is in James Robertson's books, which also contain many references for further reading:

> *The Sane Alternative: A Choice of Futures*, Robertson, revised edition, 1983.

> *Future Work: Jobs, Self-Employment and Leisure after the Industrial Age*, Gower/Temple Smith, 1985.

> *Future Wealth: A New Economics for the 21st Century*, Cassell, 1990.

The New Economics Foundation is at:

> Universal House,
> 88-94 Wentworth Street,
> London E1 7SA.

1991

THEME

WHAT FUTURE FOR
RURAL IRELAND?

SPEAKER

Michael Cuddy

Professor of Economics and Director,
Centre for Development Studies,
University College, Galway

Michael Cuddy

Economies are in a process of continual change, both sectorally and spatially. Some sectors expand, some sectors contract. Some people and some places are privileged by this change. Others are disadvantaged. Some changes take place over long, historic time periods. Others take place over shorter time horizons. There are also, of course, changes of a short-term conjunctural nature. Within the so-called democratic, capitalist system, these changes are led and dominated by market forces. Policy intervention can alter the pace and direction of this change. However, the extent to which the path, dictated by market forces, is altered depends on the political will and the financial and administrative capacity to intervene. It is well that politicians and policy makers understand these forces and processes, so that there is no illusion as to the path which society is on, and what is necessary if it wishes to change that path.

At the present time in Ireland, a particular geographical landscape has emerged, consisting of a hierarchy of urban centres and their overlapping rural hinterlands. This gives rise to a topology of rural areas, each particular rural area type being determined, primarily, by the distance from a significant urban centre. The emergence of this geographic landscape is the result of market forces within a basically capitalistic system. Economic growth has been led by the process of urbanisation. The direct result of this has been the decline of rural areas, in terms of both economic activity and population density. There is a high level of interdependence between the urban and rural. However, these various relationships are unequal ones, in favour of the urban. The urban gains at the expense of the rural.

The logic of rural decline is dictated by market forces, as economic resources and activity are sucked out of areas of dispersed population and into urban centres. The decline of the primary sectors leads rural decline in a cumulative process. Agriculture has been the most economic sector in rural areas. Through political intervention, the relative decline of this sector has been halted for a period of time, and, thereby, slowed down the decline of rural areas. However, the decision now has been taken that agriculture must re-enter the market arena and be subject to economic forces. This will hasten the decline of rural areas. As a society, we must ask whether this process of rural decline should be allowed to proceed unchecked. Should market forces continue to dictate the shape of our landscape, and the economic and social fortunes of its inhabitants? What form should intervention take? Who should intervene?

The concept 'rural' is not one which has universal acceptance. It is rather arbitrarily defined. One possible definition might run as follows. There are certain urban centres of such a size and dynamic that they are self-sustaining, that is, they continue to grow or self-generate through the operation of market forces. Geographical space beyond these spaces might be termed 'rural'. This so-called rural space is made up of functional units consisting of towns and their respective hinterlands. The economic activity in this space is multi-sectoral across the full economic spectrum. However, agriculture is traditionally important within this geographic space. The topology given in *The Future of Rural Society*, a European Commission document published in 1988, applies fairly well in Ireland. Three rural types are distinguished: the first is 'close to large urban centres and urban zones of high density economic activity experiencing overspill'; second, 'declining rural areas with significant resource base, not too far removed from the influence of large urban centres, but with significant out-migration'; and third, 'marginalised remote rural areas with little resource base, and well beyond the influence of urban centres'.

Although cities have their origins in historic factors like military strategic locations, ports, market towns, etc., the growth of cities is closely linked to economic growth, being both a cause and a result. Economic growth has been driven by urban centres, and through the operation of the powerful process of market forces. Ever since the Industrial Revolution, cities have played central roles in the development of manufacturing industry. Now, in the more industrialised countries, the tertiary or services sector is fastest growing, and it is locating primarily in urban areas. Producer services, and information technology in particular, which lead the services sector at the present time, are locating mainly in the large urban centres. In her book, *Cities and the Wealth of Nations*, on the link between city and economic growth, Jacobs argues in a most cogent and forceful fashion that cities are in fact the driving force for growth, and that regions which do not have them will not develop. By implication, rural areas which do not come under the influence of cities are destined to stagnation and decline, according to this thesis.

Urban concentration of economic activity is driven by three factors, which are central to the market economy and economic growth: concentration of product demand, external economies, and internal economies of size. Concentration of demand encourages the location of the production of final goods and services, because delivery costs to the consumer are lowered. External or agglomeration economies arise from firms locating close to each other which, in turn, generate external benefits to the firms; for example, it lowers the cost of accessing public utilities or other inputs into the production process, since there is a local concentration of demand for these inputs, thus lowering the costs of production. Internal economies arise with increasing the size of the firm. Growth of firms is facilitated by the greater ease of access to the factors of production, in particular labour and specialised labour skills.

It is precisely the advantages of urban centres which are lacking in rural areas, consequently raising production costs there and inhibiting capital investment. Thus, the market forces economic activity to locate in urban rather than in rural areas, wherever possible.

There is an unequal economic relationship between urban centres and those rural areas which lie beyond their immediate influence. Through the operation of market forces, the urban grows at the expense of rural decline. The nature of this relationship can be perceived through the examination of movements of labour, capital and goods, between urban and rural areas. Net migration takes place from rural to urban. The decision to move is the choice of private individuals and must be assumed to be based on rational choice from among the alternatives presented. This decision, however, results in a loss to the local community. There is a straight loss of investment in human capital, in the cost of raising these usually young people, including investment in their education. There is the net additional contribution which these, the most dynamic individuals, could make to local development. There is a further social loss: the very act of out-migration adds to the declining attractiveness of the local area for those who remain, which encourages further out-migration. Savings normally exceed investments in rural areas, either because the savers cannot find direct local opportunities to invest, or because local intermediary mechanisms are not in place to channel local savings into local investments. However, the overriding factor is that higher returns, with lower risk, can be had on investments in the expanding areas rather than in the contracting areas. Thus, unless there is unlimited capital availability, it will always flow from rural to expanding urban areas. As barriers to capital flows are broken down, and capital markets become more efficient and more competitive, there will always be better alternatives in the expanding urban areas.

Finally, the dominant feature of trade between urban and rural areas is that rural areas are net exporters of primary products and net importers of secondary and tertiary products: exporters of beef and dairy products, and importers of cars and television programmes. Over time, the terms of trade have gone against the primary products in all industrialised countries. Consequently, the terms of trade have gone against the rural areas over time. Rural areas must exchange increasing quantities of what they produce for any given amount which they buy in; there is a net transfer of resources from rural to urban areas. The resistance of rural areas to decline depends critically on the extent and exploitation of their indigenous resources. Primary sector activities, in particular agriculture, have traditionally been the most important contributors to the economies of rural areas.

The evolution of agriculture is very special, because of the demand/supply relationship which exists in this sector and which leads, inevitably, to its relative decline. This decline has combined with the dominating role of cities to strengthen the cumulative process in the decline of rural areas. The decline in the numbers of people engaged in agriculture in the European Community, from 20.1 million in 1965 to 9 million in 1989, clearly underlines the magnitude of the structural change which is taking place in agriculture. It represents a decline of 55 per cent in the agricultural workforce.

The path of Irish agricultural transformation has been identical to the Community change, with a decline of 53 per cent in the agricultural workforce over the same period. This exodus from agriculture further depresses demand and adversely affects employment in a wide variety of non-agricultural activities. The labour loss from agriculture thus reinforces the cumulative decline of the general economic and social fabric of rural communities. Alternative employment, created either by governments or by private firms, has proved insufficient to arrest the decline. The process of rural decline can be illustrated by the principle of circular and cumulative causation, espoused by Myrdal and others. A decline in agricultural activity reduces rural employment. This leads to out-migration, which leads to a reduction in population, and a consequent reduction in demand for local goods and services.

This, in turn, feeds back into a reduction in local employment, and the cycle continues.

Additional simultaneous factors reinforce this process. Financial and human capital outflows, combined with poor infrastructure, reduce rural employment opportunities. Out-migration depresses local social environments, which reinforces out-migration. And the nature of the out-migration is such as to leave behind an unbalanced age and sex structure, which lowers the natural population increase, which in turn further depresses population.

The process of decline in rural areas is not a uniform one. Rather, there is a graded decline, which is strongest in those areas which are most removed from large urban centres. Functions normally provided at the lower level towns and villages are moving up to higher ones, and are now no longer being provided at the lower centres; for example, schools, police stations, post offices, medical services, etc. These centres decline, and their hinterlands also decline, and so we get a hierarchy of towns and cities, where functions are moving upwards, and always the towns at the bottom of the ladder are under threat, as are their hinterlands.

The speed of rural decline has been slowed down by the operation of the Common Agricultural Policy. The nature of this policy intervention was such as inevitably to generate food surpluses. The present proposal to modify the Common Agricultural Policy, in order permanently to eliminate surpluses, will inevitably speed up the decline of rural areas unless offsetting compensations can be implemented. Also, and perhaps even more importantly, the completion of the Single European Market will intensify competition, which will further sharpen the push towards urban concentration and rural decline.

Is the outcome of this market-led process, which continuously reshapes the geographic space, and the distribution of population and economic activity within it, acceptable to the society at large? Is there any reason why policy should intervene in order to moderate this process?

There would appear to be at least two valid reasons for intervention: one is based on equity considerations; the other questions the efficacy of market forces in achieving an optimum deployment of economic activity and population in the pursuit of overall social and economic wellbeing. Structural adjustment, where some sectors and areas expand, while others contract, is the inevitable outcome of development and growth. New products and processes are discovered, through the ever-changing state of technology. This is a social phenomenon, where society in general benefits. However, society is made up of individuals, some of whom find themselves in the expanding sectors and areas, while others find themselves in the contracting sectors and areas. Both sets of people find themselves in their respective positions mainly through an accident of history.

It is not socially just, then, that those who find themselves on the crest of the wave should gain all the benefits of change, while those who find themselves in the trough should bear the economic and social costs of this change. Thus, rural areas, which find themselves on the downside of economic change, are entitled to transfers, in order that they might have access to the social and economic wellbeing and the life opportunities enjoyed by the society in general. The question which must be asked, from an economic and social point of view, is: does the process of urbanisation and rural decline give rise to a distribution of economic activity and population consistent with maximum social and economic wellbeing? In the absence of some specified social welfare function, and the means of measuring it, it is not possible to answer this question. However, it is possible to argue that market forces can push the dichotomisation of population distribution into concentration and dispersion too far. This is so because private enterprise is the dominant factor in deciding where economic activity will take place, and because of the failure of market forces to internalise to the individual enterprise certain costs and benefits generated by it.

Firms locate in larger urban centres in order to achieve the external and internal economies associated with such locations, basically reducing costs of production. They continue to locate in these centres beyond the point which is economically efficient, and therefore socially optimum, from an overall society point of view. Certain costs generated by the entry of additional firms to urban centres are borne by the state and local authorities and by individuals as private citizens. The public authorities pick up the cost of pollution and other environmental abuse, health care, crime and unemployment resulting from adverse social circumstances, and traffic congestion. Private citizens must physically and mentally endure these negative attributes, while at the same time contributing the taxes which cover the expenditures of the public authorities.

If a newly locating firm had to bear the full social cost of the impact of its decision, then it is clear that it would locate elsewhere, more likely in a smaller urban centre. Through the failure of the market mechanism to internalise costs incurred by the firm, that is, the firms paying the full social costs, there is a tendency for firms to locate in urban centres which are above the optimum size for these firms, and thus for cities to grow beyond their optimum size, at the expense of the smaller urban centres and their hinterlands. Just as the market fails to internalise the costs to firms at the upper end of the urban spectrum, it fails also to internalise, to firms at the lower end, certain social benefits. The private return to a firm locating in a smaller urban centre is very often considerably less than the social return – the return to the society as a whole. The gains to society, through the creation of a more viable community, are not internalised or do not accrue to the firm locating. This social gain, if internalised to the firm, could compensate for the overheads or diseconomies of locating in a smaller urban centre, without which the firm would not locate.

The role of labour is secondary, but no less important, in this development process. In the theoretical model of the labour market, the individual makes the employment choice, based on monetary and nonmonetary considerations. Despite a high resistance to leaving the rural area, workers are forced to move because there is no monetary return there, simply because enterprise is lacking. The worker is denied the choice of making marginal trades between the monetary and nonmonetary elements. It is a case of all or nothing: leave in order to have some monetary return, or stay and have no monetary return. Similarly, for labour employed in the urban centre which is willing to trade money for environment, the choice is a discrete one – all or nothing.

The general thesis being put forward here is that market forces are unable to allocate labour and capital optimally between urban and rural areas, and that the rural tends to be underdeveloped, while the urban is overdeveloped, at the expense of society as a whole. Decisions which are normally made by economic agents, based on private costs and benefits, do not give us the optimal social outcome. Thus, public policy must intervene in order to obtain a more socially desirable and economically optimal distribution of economic activity and population.

We turn now to intervention. First of all, it must be clear to everyone that a distinction must be made between those areas or communities which have declined, and will decline beyond survival, and those for whom all is not yet lost. For the former, intervention must, in the short term, be primarily in the context of providing access to a minimum level of economic wellbeing, which includes access to services and material goods. Within a longer term horizon, the demise of these communities must be planned in order to minimise private and social loss. For those areas which have the potential for economic and therefore social survival, two categories may be identified: those which are within the influence of self-sustaining urban centres, and those which lie beyond the immediate influence of such centres.

For these rural areas, there are at least two intervention strategies for rural development which should be implemented. One is global in its application; the other is local. If the thesis on the role of cities in economic growth is correct, then a policy of urban distribution is an essential element of an effective rural development strategy. This comes within the ambit of regional development policy. The central objective here must be to restrict the growth of those urban centres where diseconomies or further industrial locations are clearly evident, and simultaneously to privilege the smaller urban centres, so that they can reach a level where they are self-sustaining. The increase in the number of self-sustaining urban centres will thus contribute to the stabilisation of a wider rural hinterland. This policy should be effected by insisting that firms locating in the larger urban centres bear the full social location costs, while firms locating in the smaller centres should reap the full benefits of their social contribution.

The local focus must be a development strategy which exploits the local indigenous resources and generates ancillary activities in order to maximise local value added. A local development strategy is not a new concept in Ireland. However, traditionally, it has remained rudimentary in nature and has not extended significantly beyond a collection of mainly social initiatives. One reason for this has been the lack of any official recognition or public support for local development groups. Local communities lacked the technical capacity and institutional support, as well as lacking integration into the larger planning structure, all of which was necessary in order to achieve any notable success. Recognition, though, has finally been given to the legitimacy and the necessity to plan at the local level. This is primarily due to the instigation of the European Community Commission. A bottom-up integrated approach, across sectors and instruments, is the preferred scenario of the EC Commission at this time. It is the approach which was advocated, but not adopted, in the application of the recent reform of structural funds in Ireland. It is the approach being insisted on now in the implementation of the Leader Programme, which is the EC-funded local area-based development initiative. However, local area planning will only be successful if it is integrated into the larger planning process at regional, national and European Community level.

The effect of exploitation of indigenous resources can only be achieved if the various obstacles to their exploitation are removed. The required actions include: human resource enhancement, infrastructure development, the mobilisation of local savings and external capital, and the putting in place of the appropriate administration structures.

There is a hierarchy of actors associated with the development of rural areas, extending from the European Community down to the local community. Each tier in the hierarchy has the responsibility, and the capacity, to fulfil its particular role in supporting and promoting the development process. It is here that the concept of subsidiarity finds its true expression. Rural development is about raising the socioeconomic wellbeing of people in local communities. The ultimate responsibility for the livelihood of individuals and their families must rest with the individuals themselves, in their own work situations, in various types of employment and entrepreneurial roles. The first level of organised support in achieving economic development at the local level is the collective action of the local community in setting its goals and priorities and mapping out an action path to achieve its targets. It can collectively help to overcome certain obstacles to development at the local level. In particular, it can draw on the regional and state support apparatus and institutions to overcome these obstacles.

Local community action can be carried out in various ways – through local elected authorities, as is normally the case in mainland Europe; through organised voluntary bodies or co-operatives, as is traditionally the case in Ireland; through the so-called 'third sector' companies, which are receiving certain acclaim in Ireland at the present time; or some combination of these various approaches. If, however, the local community fails to organise itself through the absence of appropriate administrative structure, or if it cannot be stimulated or motivated into organisation in order to support local development, then the demise of that community has already commenced. If the local community cannot, for whatever reason, take some of the initiative and responsibility for its own affairs, its own future, it is unlikely that any outside agency or authority can, or will.

There is a key role to be played by regional authorities in the research and planning of development, based on the region's strengths, co-ordinating and supporting local developmental strategies and co-ordinating the implementation of national and EC policy at that level. However, Ireland lacks the political maturity to put in place such regional structures. Politicians have been dissuaded by civil servants from putting such structures in place; not through any objective planning reasons, but because they do not have confidence in the ability of lesser beings to achieve what they themselves have yet to achieve; because they are preoccupied with financial control at all costs; or because they fear, simply, the shock to the existing conservative organisational system which change would generate. One so-called objective reason for lack of regionalisation of planning in Ireland has been that Ireland, as a whole, stands to gain more transfers from the European Community through our present single-region status. This claim, which has never been demonstrated, must be seriously questioned, and the real reasons interrogated. If the claim could be substantiated, the dynamic released through the regionalisation in the promotion of regional and national growth would seem significantly to outweigh any marginal financial transfers from the Community through a single-region status.

The role of national government within this hierarchy must comprise national planning and priority setting, including fiscal, monetary, sectoral, regional and infrastructural policies.

There are, however, two key areas which are critical to rural development and for which national government has responsibility. The first is the putting in place of the appropriate national, regional and local administrative structures, through which the different level players in the hierarchy can exercise their full roles. The second is in relation to regional policy, and in particular the structure of the urban system. Unfortunately, with respect to urban distribution, the national government has only a limited capacity to affect this, since this particular stage has moved on from being national to being more an international one. Because of the internationalisation of markets, and the inability of individual governments to influence certain international factors which have an important impact on the national territory, the European Community has an increasingly significant role to play in national, regional and, therefore, rural development policy. In particular, the policy of urban distribution, throughout the Community, is increasingly an issue which can only be effectively addressed at the level of the Community. In fact, Ireland, as a peripheral region within the larger Community, is increasingly dependent on the latter's policies for its social and economic wellbeing. If Ireland does not get the sort of consideration within the Community that the regions within Ireland should have got within the national administration, then Ireland will experience a relative decline within the Community, similar to the decline experienced by the peripheral regions within Ireland.

Because of its narrow economic base, Ireland has not got the financial capacity, within a medium-term timeframe, to move the economy towards providing the living standards enjoyed by the Community as a whole. The continuing budgetary crisis is just the symptom of the underlying relative weakness of our overall national economy. Furthermore, our incapacity to research, plan and implement effective political, administrative and support structures is a by-product of our relative economic poverty. We are incapable of breaking this vicious circle. Therefore, we need the Community to at least share these tasks with us.

So, where does rural Ireland go? Rural Ireland is already in a depressed state. This is the logical outcome of the operation of the market forces in the larger capitalist society. It will, inevitably, come under increasing pressure with the proposed reduction in the Common Agricultural Policy supports, and the creation of the Single European Market. Rural development is primarily spatial in character. It has a particular sectoral dimension, which is agriculture. However, the latter is of secondary importance, I believe, and will become even less important over time in the determination of the viability of rural communities. The future of rural areas is clearly tied to the future of regional development within Ireland, and especially in the European Community. The role of urban centres, and their distribution, is critical to the destiny of rural areas. This will depend less and less on factors within Ireland, but rather on the ability of the European Community to regulate urban concentration and the distribution of economic activity within the Community as a whole.

A second major element in determining the future of rural areas is the capacity to plan and process economic development from the bottom up. This requires, *inter alia*, the putting in place of administrative structures, from local level through to the level of the European Community, passing through regional and national structures. This is necessary so that each level in the hierarchy can engage in, and discharge, those responsibilities which are within its competence.

A third element which will determine the future of rural Ireland is the financial capacity to put in place the supporting structures, both physical and non-physical. The financial capacity of Ireland to do this is rather limited, because of its small economic base. It therefore depends on the generosity or the self-interest, and the importance of Ireland to that self-interest, of the European Community. The latter, however, is under increasing pressure financially, through its support for the development of Eastern Europe. This poses a threat to releasing Ireland from its current position on the economic treadmill. The economic and social future of Ireland cannot be distinguished from the future of Ireland and its regions together. The future of both depends on the capacity to formulate and implement development policies within Ireland, and on the evolving relationship between Ireland and the European Community. However, it is imperative that Irish society, and in particular its politicians, are aware of what sort of rural landscape the unfettered market forces will realise, and it is also important that they realise how they must intervene in order to modify this evolution. But, first of all, it is necessary to create and make explicit the desired vision of the future rural society, the future rural Ireland: what would they like it to look like? This is where the debate should start in Ireland. This is the debate, I believe, which must be taken to Europe.

1992

THEME

EDUCATION FOR FREEDOM

SPEAKER

Michael D Higgins

Lecturer in Political Science and Sociology,
University College Galway,
poet, Labour TD for Galway West,
Minister for Arts, Culture and the Gaeltacht 1992-1997

Michael D Higgins

The Delivery

I have delivered my children
to school
in the half grey light.
Always,
the half grey light
reminds me
of anxious arrivals,
temporary releases.
Hurried half kisses
furtively offered
must be sufficient
for that time
of the offering up.

Leaving
I question my complicity
No blind faith any longer
moves me.
I am the deliverer
of what were my children
to the Chapel of fear
for sacrifice.
I weep full tears,
alone.

(From *The Season of Fire*)

There are few subjects as important as education. For some, it is the route to escape; for others, ascent along a meritocratic ladder; for others, a prerequisite for the acquisition of wealth; for so many, a bad memory; for those fortunate to have encountered inspired teachers, a warm memory.

Yet it is central, not only to our existence and our ability to be human, but to the development of that capacity for future generations. Put simply, the interaction between education, economy and society has not only an immediate importance. That interaction determines the reproduction and shapes the responses to change in society.

Yet on that interaction, there are so many questions that rarely get asked.

When parents send their children to school any morning, how much are they allowed to know about that to which they send their children? How democratic is their education? How possible is it for teachers as professionals to review and renew their capacity in their subjects? Can education be joyful? Is it democratic or republican to reject political and social literacy in the widest sense, to refuse to teach political and social studies in the curriculum, while piously looking for a committed citizenry? Above all, is education to be allowed to facilitate changes in the direction of that more human world we have scarcely dreamed of, or is education condemned to respond, react to change as such change is interpreted by narrow vested interests?

I have been asked all of these questions in recent times. I welcome that and my response is, let us begin such a Great Debate in education as will engage these and other questions.

Recent decades have shown a great imprecision, and an even greater distrust, of language. I sense, regularly now, a feeling that all meaning is arbitrary, that concepts such as democracy, equality, freedom, justice, rights are as often employed as terms of abuse as they are as tools of understanding. Indeed, one could go further and say that understanding the world has quite declined as an intellectual project by comparison with controlling the world, or of imposing on the world a single, or more usually, economic, version of itself.

Freedom has been defined and reduced to market freedom. Equality has been pilloried as the pursuit, a jealous pursuit at that, of sameness. Justice has been sacrificed again and again as it is limited and equated with legal process. Individuals and families, whole societies have been destroyed in this distinction. Democracy itself has been limited to the few occasions when parliament is elected. It has been excluded almost as a moral principle, it seems at times, from the social and economic world. In foreign policy, theories based on democracy and right have been replaced by a theory of interest. Democracy has not been allowed to extend into, and permeate, our lives.

Yet, in a time of broken words and an uncertain world, the irrepressible search for authenticity, authenticity of self, of class, of nation, of humanity, continues. Within that search I believe that the role of education is crucial and must now be debated in a context sufficiently wide to question all those themes that have been evaded until now.

Indeed, it ill behoves a country such as Ireland that now calls itself a republic, and that was established through the courage of those who had so much less than most of us, to be content that the prevailing version of ourselves must constitute, in educational thinking, the borrowed failed ideas of our former coloniser, founded on their concession and legacy, reformed on their failed initiatives. Why not make a start even now at something original and creative?

To begin with some basic principles: I have learned with pain to recognise the difference between schooling and education. I have had to face the reality that, as a parent, I could not be clear as to whether I was delivering my children to a public school, a national school or a denominational school. I realised that even in the systematic evasion of the question of control, a great rejection of democracy and republicanism was involved. I wrote the poem with which I opened in a black moment, when it struck me that far from joy displacing dreariness that so many recall, children in the future were to be made the pawns of a new version of education such as is outlined in the recent Green Paper, that denied creativity as strongly as it demanded from even the earlier levels of education the dehumanising values of Von Hayek, borrowed by Friedmann, and used as tools of oppression by the administrations of Margaret Thatcher and Ronald Reagan, and brought home to Ireland from the British jumble sale of ideas by the insecure followers of acquisitive greed, rather than proponents of creativity and joy.

No one could be as long as I am in politics without noting the unequal distribution of resources that has affected access to education. Let me emphasise one fundamental point: until a movement commences aimed at enshrining education as a right, we will never redress the inbuilt inequalities of our system.

Beyond the issues of control and access there have been even fewer opportunities to discuss curriculum.

It is in this latter neglect that perhaps most is revealed. Curriculum provokes such questions as: What is being taught? For what purpose? For whose benefit? It exposes the connections between society, economy and education. Even well-intentioned people have become so worn out on extending the quantity of education that they have been left so exhausted as never to reach the issue of the quality or content of education.

Some writers recently have gone so far as to assert that education, because of the volume of spending involved, must justify itself in meeting the needs of the economy, and the domestic economy at that. I refer of course to the supporting volume on education of the recent *Culliton Report*.

There is a shabbiness to the arguments that have followed the publication of such views that is only exceeded by the silence of those who are yet to speak. I do hope that the challenge and example of such educationalists as Dr Pádraig

Hogan is emulated. His paper, 'The Sovereignty of Learning, the Fortunes of Schooling and the new Educational Virtuousness',[1] is a seminal contribution. May it and the efforts of parents, teachers and administrators force the pace and give us the adequate education debate we need, a debate that would indeed deserve the title The Great Education Debate.

That debate must include the issues of Control, Access and Curriculum. Such a debate too will have to be inclusive rather than exclusive. There will have to be respect for the opinions of all on such questions as, What is democracy in education? What is authoritarianism in Irish Education? In education in general? How can democracy be made to prevail? There are some who are happy to have education run in an authoritarian way. Let's hear from them. Theirs is a most unusual view, to be content to have education function as an autocratic undemocratic institutional structure within a formal democracy and a rhetorical republic.

Of course, it is never put like that. In educational matters, there is an official or formal transcript, but there is also a separate transcript of practice. Quiet capitulation, moral acquiescence prevails, but, I ask, where in the world have patriarchy or authoritarianism as personality traits disappeared by a quiet evolution, other than by being named, acknowledged, and then, by democratic decision, abandoned?

The silent who morally acquiesce are victims in charge of future victims, handing on from generation to generation that moral acquiescence as a substitute for participatory citizenship.

Silence must be broken. The challenge to those who have been silent up to now on the shape of education in the future is to confront those who would see education in the future as enjoying a minor functional relationship to the prevailing economic prejudices of the day and, let's admit it, to economic ideas that have failed, and that have often been based on

---

[1] Ó hÓgáin, Pádraig (1992) *British Journal of Educational Studies*, vol. XXXX, no. 2, pp. 134-148.

exploitation. In this usage, 'prevailing economic prejudices', I make the distinction between such and the theoretically grounded antecedents of such aberrations that exist in the history of what was once called Political Economy.

Political Economy was, in the classical period of economic thought, seen as an instrument of a moral purpose, a philosophical purpose.

I was asked to give this lecture not long after I had been making a documentary film on the United Nations Conference on Environment and Development (UNCED) in Rio de Janeiro earlier this year. In preparing for that task, I had gone back to material from authors such as Gregory Bateson and Fritjof Capra.[2] I recalled being struck by the starkness of the choice they provoked, when I wrote in 1972 of such writers.[3] They quoted the assumptions of the Idea of Progress based on such propositions as: 'It's us against Nature.' The alternative assumption was, 'It's us in symmetry with and as part of Nature.' The first assumption was enforced through colonialism and imperialism. In my own schooling, it was represented by the modernisation model, the ideological glasses placed on all of us scholars from the so-called developing world who studied in the US in the 1960s and which had the effect of blinding us to the reality of our own story when we returned home from the metropolitan centre of thought. The second assumption was and is a fundamental of the thinking of the Eastern thought influencing the rising ecological consciousness of that time. At Rio, even the most tough-minded followers of the old Idea of Progress were forced to admit that development was not open-ended in an ecological sense. In the same period as the reassertion of ecological responsibility, the feminist movement has made even greater advances. In the south of the planet, where four-fifths of the planet's population are allowed

---

[2]   Bateson, Gregory. *Steps towards an Ecology of Mind.* Capra, Fitjof, *The Tao of Physics: The Turning Point.*

[3]   Higgins, Michael D (1972) 'The marvellous symmetry of the Universe', *Education Times.*

less than one-fifth of the world's resources, aid, trade and debt are being explored by a new generation of economists, social scientists, political scientists, lawyers, educated often in exile, tortured at home, but close to the needs and democratic aspirations of their own people.

The formal rhetoric of the UNCED never engaged this new and creative thinking.

The rejection had less to do with the distinction between head and heart than to the difference between the 'public transcript of powerful nations and the public transcript of dependent nations', as James C Scott put it.[4]

The private transcripts were there too with all their ringing challenge.

Let me say a little about this concept of transcripts. Scott gives the story of Aggy as recounted in Albert J Raboteau's *Slave Religion: The 'Invisible Institution' of the Antebellum South*.[5]

Aggy's daughter has been beaten for a crime of which she was innocent. Aggy is forced to look on, but, left alone in the slave living quarters, she is visited by the governess, Mary Livermore, and she bursts out:

> 'Thar's a day a-comin'! Thar's a day a-comin'!
> ... I hear the rumblin' ob de chariots! I see de
> flashin' ob de guns! White folks' blood is a
> runnin' on the ground like a ribber, an de dead's
> heaped up dat high! ... Oh Lor! Hasten de day
> when de blows, an de bruises, and de aches an de
> pains, shall come to de white folks, an de buzzards
> shall eat dem as dey's dead in de streets. Oh Lor!
> Roll on de chariots, an gib the black people rest
> and peace. Oh Lor! Gib me de pleasure ob livin'
> till dat day, when I shall see white folks shot down

---

[4] Scott, James C (1990) *Domination and the Arts of Resistance.* Yale University Press.

[5] *Ibid.*, pp. 4-5, reference to quotation in 'My Story of the War', in Raboteau.

like de wolves when dey come hungry out o' de
woods.'[6]

Those who dominate have a public transcript for public
consumption and a private one for consumption in the security
of their own company. George Orwell's dilemma recounted
in *Shooting an Elephant* is used by Scott to illustrate this.[7]
The dominated too have a public transcript; it is one of
deference. Scott quotes the old Ethiopian proverb: 'When the
great lord passes, the wise peasant bows deeply and farts'.[8]
The dominated also have a private transcript, and they well
up in themselves frustration, rage, a memory, a legacy of wrong
and exclusion. The dam breaks on all these emotions at the
moment of liberation or even of rumour of the possibility of
liberation.

I wonder how many private transcripts there are buried
beneath the formal public transcript of deference that is
demanded from institutionalised education and those who have
had it forced on them, those who have been forced to exist
within it? How many speeches have been rehearsed in silent
rage, and, to the untold damage of those who composed them,
never been delivered?

How valuable it would be if The Great Debate began with
a great breaking of silence on all of the issues, including the
ones I have listed.

When, in a radio programme entitled *My Education*, I said,
among other things, and with enthusiasm, 'I feel my education
is only beginning at 50', I seemed to strike a note of resonance
with a very disparate but open-minded community of listeners.[9]

What I had in mind was that I was in a curious, maybe even
desperate, way attempting a kind of search for a fantasy home

---

[6] Scott, *op. cit.*, p. 6.

[7] *Ibid.*, pp. 10-11.

[8] *Ibid.*, Title page.

[9] *My Education*, RTÉ Radio 1, 1992. Published in: Quinn, John (ed.)
     (1997) *My Education*. Dublin: Town House.

where true education was possible. Let me say immediately
that I do not believe it is possible, sufficient, maybe even
desirable, that I should know whether such a home in the sense
of a settled place, or a defined period of time, ever existed; if
it did, where it was located and how I might make my way
there. My life has been enriched by uncertainty that, even if it
has brought pain, has brought openness, my battered
philosophical suitcase.

What might be more appropriate, it seemed to me, was to
attempt a journey along a curve, a heroic journey that, if
completed, might bring one home even in dream or an old
psychic harmony to a harmonious unity, where one could
experience the shared breath of the planet. But then again,
'home' might turn out to be a formidable and challenging
illusion.

When one is a young scholar, one is always made insecure,
the peasant not ready for the parlour. When you are an older
scholar, you are seduced towards becoming secure, an
institutionalised piece of furniture in the parlour, cynical, but,
in my own case, desperately anxious to begin again and again
and again, radically rooted in the experience and history of
one's human companions and their concerns. The quest for
authenticity in life and language is certain to bring pain and
can make no certain guarantees, only a possibility, of a moment
of joy, of celebration of the Divinity of total undivided
humanity. Yet it is the fundamental quest.

On my journey along the curve of old questions and books
revisited, authors that I would like to call, with respect to
Gurdgieff, *Meetings with Remarkable Ghosts,* came forward.
Among the most important was Hannah Arendt. I encountered
her through Melvyn A Hill's *Hannah Arendt: The Recovery
of the Public World.*[10] In that volume I was intrigued by both
the cover photograph of Hannah Arendt with a cigarette

---

[10] Hill, Melvyn A (ed.) (1979) *Hannah Arendt: The Recovery of the Public
World.* New York: St Martin's Press.

perilously close to the hair above her left ear, a gesture of addiction, anxiety, vulnerability, or was it employed as an aid to concentration? And Glenn Gray's chapter, 'The abyss of freedom and Hannah Arendt'.[11]

The photograph revealed in Hannah Arendt's face the terrible problem of choice and individuation. The phrase 'the abyss of freedom' encapsulated for me the central moral issue of this century. In her uncompleted final work, Hannah Arendt drew a distinction between thinking, willing and judging. The set of lectures on the first was completed. Preparation of the second set of lectures caused her great problems. She died before the lectures for the third topic were completed.

For her, freedom was exercised through thinking. But that was not enough.

For educational theory, the lesson is that we have to educate for both the integral personality and the social self.

Hannah Arendt asserted that, if we were to avoid the impasse, the moral loneliness and angst of the isolated ego, we must be 'able to do what we ought to will'. 'To be able to do what we ought to will' – in this is a powerful agenda for education.[12] We are called to act as well as to will. Our action, as she develops it further, is also social or communal, not isolated.

Between the photo and the article too, I felt a sense of pain, a pain I have come to know of the private person impelled across this bridge of consciousness to the realm of the public. Hannah Arendt wrote:

> Even those among us who by speaking and writing have ventured into public life have not done so out of any original pressure in the public scene and have hardly expected, or aspired, to

---

[11] *Ibid.*, pp. 225-245, G Glenn Gray, 'The abyss of freedom and Hannah Arendt', in Hill, Melvyn A (ed.) (1979) *Hannah Arendt: The Recovery of the Public World.* New York: St Martin's Press.

[12] *Ibid.*, p. 229.

receive the stamp of public approval ... these efforts were, rather, guided by their hope of preserving some minimum of humanity in a world grown inhuman while, at the same time, as far as possible, resisting the weird unreality of this worldlessness – each after his own fashion and some few by seeking to the limits of their ability to understand even inhumanity and the intellectual and political monstrosities of a time out of joint.[13]

What a contemporary challenge that is to all those in education.

I feel here that what is at stake is, maybe, more than the solipsistic agony of a self alone, fashioned out of will. There is the as yet unchallenged burden of knowing, a stage beyond thought, will and judgement, a stage where instinct and the heart force on the rational an impulse to action that makes it not only uncomfortable, but impossible for thought to be a mere spectator in the game of life.

G Glenn Gray acknowledges, too, Arendt's category of contingency. He gives as example the experience of the artist who succeeds by willing success, often against failure. She or he has seen success in achieving the finished symbolic object in their 'mind's eye'.[14]

Isn't it interesting that creativity and the arts were the single greatest omission in the recent Green Paper? How long, I ask, can we live in a political system where the institution of education is precluded from taking responsibility for political and philosophical, critical thought, and yet at the same time another more generally consumed institution, the media, frequently equates public life with venality, corruption and self-seeking? Why not make it possible for millions to be educated in ethical, political, philosophical alternatives and

---

[13] *Ibid.*, p. 294, Melvyn A Hill, 'The fictions of mankind and the stories of men', in Hill, Melvyn A (ed.) (1979) *Hannah Arendt: The Recovery of the Public World.* New York: St Martin's Press.

[14] Melvyn A Hill, *op. cit.*, p. 238.

let them all sweep in to debate, to participate, to initiate and to create change?

Is it not the protection of unquestionable certainties that lies at the root of this cancer of exclusion and alienation?

Have we seen what a democratic education would be, even in our 'mind's eye'? We will always be strung out on the challenge of a world in which, by one excess, we could be consumed by a reality never known, or on the other, we could perish by our being repelled from the world. As I was preparing this lecture, I saw a documentary on Thomas Merton. How well Merton understood the poles of the dilemma, more importantly, the need to recognise their challenge.

Education is inescapably located in a context of continually challenging forms of life and unresolved philosophical challenges. Education is not some form of commodity or utility which we can measure in terms only of quantity or setting – although any government that condemns pupils to lesser involvement, and teacher and pupils to insanitary and drab buildings, is disqualifying itself from measurement as a democratic administration.

Education is inescapably about the integrity of the learner, the evolution of the teacher, the moral growth of both, in a complex, ever more interdependent, world. Parents are living, making and shaping that world too. Often they are mutilated within it and yearn for another more human form of society, even if it will be for their children and not themselves.

Yet, back from Rio, not one significant theme from ecology, feminism, egalitarianism, cultural pluralism ... could I find in the framework for the Great Debate in Education. Yet the values of antisocial, aggressive, individualist greed – core values of Thatcher-Reaganism – were there beneath a thin veneer of 'corporate speak'.

Rejected entirely was any debate, so central to educational theory, on the nature of creativity. It is crucial if we accept creativity as social, rather than inherently a private attribute, that we make it a central informing principle of curriculum. Otherwise, we are left with the alternative of privately purchased units of child improvement, imposed on children outside the school day. How well I remember it! 'The piano will stand to her', and the role of parents sending, delivering, collecting and, of course, paying. Worst of all, children whose parents cannot afford it are excluded from all the developmental potential of the arts.

In a world where the impact of science and technology in the interests of an economics of acquisitive greed has done so much ecological damage as to warrant the leaders of the world to come together, where consciousness itself is inadequate, and language emptying of meaning, must we not demand that our children's creativity and humanness be allowed to flower so that, in the next century, our planet will be peopled by those who think holistically and have been allowed to develop the mind of peace informed by hearts where love, and the will to take on the responsibility of interdependency, can reside? Any education towards freedom requires that future children, ourselves, returning, continuing, retired students, have the freedom to go on past the rut of our existence and the thought imposed on us, or deprived from us, or not dreamed of yet.

I want, this evening, to list some personal themes about which I would love to hear during the Great Educational Debate.

They are only samples. Please, do not inundate me with obvious omissions. What is the difference, I ask myself, at fifty-one, between a pedagogy of fear and a pedagogy of love?

Son of a peasant, I have felt, so often, like a migrant in the metropolis as I made my way past the excluding and often intimidating signposts of postgraduate seminars – in three university systems. What little excitement there was of the sharing of knowledge, or even commitment to such a project, what minimal patience, what absence of generosity … In another culture, post-dictatorship Nicaragua, I saw and tried to learn that powerful generosity of defining education as the sharing of stories and dreams, of respecting energetic curiosity, above all of education for true participation and effective citizenship, from such people as the brothers Ernesto and Fernando Cardenal. And I have wept for all the children humiliated, mocked, and in the past beaten, made insecure by such systems as substituted the agenda of order for the aims of leading out the inner light of every wonderful person. This, for me, is neither idealistic or sentimental. It is an issue of rights, rather like the abolition of slavery. It is an insult to the intelligence to suggest that an authoritarian regime is a necessary condition for effective administration in education.

A pedagogy of love would eschew fear as a principle of education. We are far from a general beginning, not to speak of the completion of such a project. To be accurate, it has been begun in brave and isolated places, and has been sustained, unevenly, and against the odds.

What are the prospects then of education for peace? Of educating for participation, of educating for creative co-operation? What is the likelihood of our becoming critical participants in the debate on the connection between science, technology and society? What will be our opportunities for constructing a curriculum where there could be a respect for the right of all peoples to tell their story and have their dreams regarded with respect?

In this country for whose liberation my father, a man of limited education, but who possessed the courage to embrace a project that transcended his and his fellow apprentices' self-interest, fought to make free, these questions I have listed. Formal if not intellectual independence, having been gained, have not been allowed to surface. They have been buried or evaded by lesser people, terrified and timid people, people threatened by nothing more than clerical displeasure or seduced by meritocratic individualism. They drifted on with educational directives, illegally some would say, in the 20th century, happy with the colonisers' 19th century sop, and later their outmoded, dated version of education. That they sacrificed democratic education, or education for democracy, did not, and some would say does not, bother them.

Now, late in the 20th century, their heirs ask us to forget the world and settle for the real but limited project of being citizens of a European Economic Union, rather than the great transcendental challenge of being human in the most international and interdependent sense of that term. They ask us to be useful to a dying economic system, rather than inviting us to be allies in building a new, just, peaceful, interdependent, international economic and social order. We must surrender our lives and our children's lives, the lives of the planetary family, to dying and dead ideas. We must surrender our capacity to produce ideas and will new creative versions of society.

Most recently, education has been constituted a commodity. A teacher is to become an executive. A university president is to envisage himself, or, in the unlikely event, herself, as 'the chief executive of a multi-million pound company', I read recently in a Dáil speech in defence of the Green Paper.[15]

If neo-utilitarianism gives content to the public transcript of education and if the alternative, private up to now, transcripts do not move quickly to confrontation, there will be a terrible harvest to reap … and it will not be within the same terms of discourse, perhaps thinly veiled, that are available now.

I have consistently supported the late Raymond Williams' proposals for curriculum reform in his day. For English conditions, he suggested, for example, a curriculum that would include:

1. Extensive practice in the fundamental languages of English and Maths.

2. General knowledge of ourselves and our environment.

3. History and criticism of literature, the visual arts, music, dramatic performance, landscape and architecture.

---

[15] Dáil Debates, October 1992.

4. Extensive practice in democratic procedures and practice in the use of libraries, newspapers and magazines, radio and TV programmes and other sources of information, opinion and influence.

5. Introduction to at least one other culture, including its language, history, geography, institutions and arts, to be given in part by visiting and exchange.

I recall the more ambitious aims of Quentin Hoare who felt that Williams' reforms required a socialist transformation of teachers and society that Williams, he felt, neglected.

Hoare gave four distinguishing marks for a socialist approach:

1. Critical, as opposed to conservative tradition, it would stress education as the development of critical reason in the child, questioning alternatives to all existing reality.

2. As opposed to the Romantic School, it would embody a full acceptance of the social character of humanity, rejecting forever the notion of a pre-social dimension of human existence – the image of Emile.

3. As opposed to rationalisation, it would insist on the active nature of children's participation in the learning process and contest the mechanist concept of education as transmission of fixed skills.

4. As opposed to democratic tradition, it would be dialectical, treating all human reality as radically historical, refusing to consider programmes outside man's capacity to execute, emasculate or refuse them.[16]

That was all so long ago. It may surprise some of you to hear that I would protect education's freedom not to be ever forced to serve any particular ideology. Rather, I would want it to be free to develop critical thought in the best sense of that term. I would be with Raymond Williams rather than Quentin Hoare.

---

[16] Hoare, Quentin (1977) 'Education: programmes and people', in Martin Hayles (ed.) *The Politics of Literacy*, pp. 48-49. London: Writers and Readers Publishing Co-operative.

Since then, other themes have arrived, including the ecological challenge and the threatened loss of the human population of whole continents such as Africa, of their capacity for food security, their position made fragile by the $55 billion transferred each year from South to North. At this moment, we are facing the choice of a new relationship to the planet and each other. We can educate for regression to brutal self-interest or we can educate for peace and true security, for openness.

What is required now is a critical capacity developed within an educational system where creativity is made central.

We should not despair. We should remember Russell:

> Meantime, the world in which we exist has other aims. But it will pass away, burned up in the fire of its own hot passions; and from its ashes will spring a new and younger world, full of fresh hope, with the light of morning in its eyes.[17]

If we engage the connections between science, technology and society, it is possible for us, even yet, to become a symbol-using, rather than a symbol-abusing, species, and to experience the joy of our humanness, made immanent.

It is possible for us, as Raymond Williams put it, to be the arrow not the target, within the technology of television and culture.[18]

Let us choose then the pedagogy of love. Let us allow the pedagogy of fear to fall away from our institutions, our practice and our personalities.

Let us make education a right, accessible through one's entire life.

Let us have real democracy, elective and accountable, not only in a geographical sense, but in a community sense. Let us elect our representatives for educational accountability from

---

[17] Quoted in Noam Chomsky, *Problems of Knowledge and Freedom*, p. 83, quoting Bertrand Russell.

[18] The title of his lecture to the Festival of Celtic Film.

within the sectors involved and from outside. Why should we settle for less, unless we are conceding democracy itself?

The new dawn of which Russell wrote will only be possible if we refuse to surrender education to the passing fad of neo-utilitarianism.

In the next century, we will be asked to be many things but, above all, we will be most useful to the human family and ourselves if we are holistic.

I am mindful of the issue of resources for education. I have supported and will support the political fight for adequate resources and their direction, in particular, to areas of disadvantage. But we do not have to choose between activity on that issue and related issues, such as in-service training and renewal, and we can no longer neglect the debate about the very nature of education itself.

In conclusion, then, may I say that there is too much that is covert in Irish education. There is far too much piecemeal decision-making. The antipathy to intellectual ideas, to philosophy and theory in education, and in the social sciences in general, must be ended.

For example, so many within teaching, so many parents, would welcome a debate on education's place in a New World Communicative Order.

They would welcome too the tension between the control functions of education and its responsibilities for enhancing and releasing creativity, being set in tension and such tension being critically examined.

It is a time for courage, a time to demand and ensure that, in our country, education will never again be allowed to destroy the wonderment of a child. Rather that, heroically, we will begin to make our way back to that wonderment and live in peace with each other and our planet.

If educating towards freedom means discomfort, let's choose it, consciously, as an alternative to giving the control and content of education away, or, more abject still, 'morally acquiescing' by our silence in what is the substitute for building democratic education and education for democracy.

We are not asked to pay the price of Aggy the Slave. We can and should exercise our democracy and, by making education genuinely democratic, at last set out on one of the obvious heroic journeys of an authentic republic.

Within that great national journey we can all make personal journeys to wholeness, people in solidarity within a great movement of planetary and social healing.

Let me end as I began with a poem written from the broken pieces of my own life, a poem for my youngest son. I dedicate it to parents, teachers and satchel-kickers everywhere …

Collecting

As my eyes peel the playground,
I am distracted
by sounds that are chaotic,
celebrations of release.
The harness of satchels
is being tossed
with a disrespect
hard-earned.

The bag, discarded,
is placed in perspective
by an involuntary kick
from a stranger
who had not invested it
with the intimacies
of welts and warm shoulders.
It is the peopled yard
that attracts
the backward glance.

The class-rooms, abandoned,
linger in empty silence
until morning
when the breath of authority
will again define
their arbitrary purpose.

Their long shadow
captures the first words,
'I've a pile of homework.'
We drive on homewards
with the wedge of school between us.

(From *The Season of Fire*)

One day children will come to school and the day will begin with music and they will learn in relaxation. Fear abandoned, love will define the pedagogic process. We must make that day.

1993

THEME

A WEE STORY FROM ENNISKILLEN

SPEAKER

Gordon Wilson

*An 'ordinary wee draper' from Enniskillen,
whose suffering in the Enniskillen bombing of
November 1987 led him to work tirelessly for peace
until his death in 1995,
former member of Seanad Éireann*

Gordon Wilson

I have to say this: this is not the story of Enniskillen; this is simply a story from Enniskillen. But, having said that, I do not forget that ten other lovely gentle people died in that bomb, and that now over three thousand people have died in Northern Ireland in the last twenty-five years, and that forty thousand people are injured, as the result of terrorism. But I do not speak for them; I speak for me and mine.

A little about my family background. I was born in 1927, in a little place called Manorhamilton in the County Leitrim, in the Republic. I was the first of four children, with three younger sisters. Eight hundred souls, and seventeen pubs. I was born into a 5 per cent Protestant minority, but we didn't have any community relations officers in Manorhamilton, because we didn't need them. The communities got on well with each other, we trusted each other, we respected each other. My father came from some two miles out of town; his people were farming people. You will know that the land in Leitrim is perhaps the worst in Ireland. Four of the six in my father's family emigrated; there just wouldn't have been a living for them. The farm was at the bottom of a mountain, and if ever I get a little uppity at home, and it happens sometimes, my wife is quick to remind me that I come from the bottom of a mountain in the bogs of Leitrim. And if I get very uppity indeed, as sometimes happens, she will mention the name of the particular bog, and that brings me back to earth. My father came into one of the three local drapery shops to serve his apprenticeship. In a town of eight hundred people with three drapery shops, they were not big shops. He bought the shop in 1925, and he married my mother in 1926. She was a nurse. She was from Ballykelly, in the County Derry, four miles down the road from Greysteel.

We had a happy home. We lived over the shop and, of course, life revolved around the shop and our church. I went to the local primary school, the Masterson Primary School. Thirty-five Protestant young people, one teacher – the principal, a Mrs Boyd who was an Irish language fanatic. She was a good teacher, but she was a hard woman. She had an ash plant at the side door and she used it liberally. Many's the time I got my bottom warmed, whether I was innocent or guilty, and not a bit of harm it did me. Those days are gone.

In 1939, two days after the war broke out, I, as a ten-year-old cub from Leitrim, in short trousers, was sent to Wesley College, a Methodist boarding and day school for boys and girls, then in Stephen's Green in Dublin – now it's in Dundrum. You can perhaps imagine the shock it was for me coming from Leitrim at ten years of age, leaving home and into the big time, in the big city. On the night that I arrived in Wesley, I was told, like all the others, to report to the office of the vice-principal, a Mr McDowell, and I did. Having established my identity, he said to me: 'Tell me, Wilson, are you a Protestant or a Presbyterian?' And entering into what I thought was the spirit of the evening, I said: 'Neither, sir. I'm a Methodist.' Mac, as we called him, was not amused. He wasn't into scoring draws, and certainly not with brats of cubs of ten years of age.

I spent six years in Dublin – the war years; I heard my first bombs drop in Dublin, on the night that the Germans bombed Dublin. I did my Leaving Cert. and just passed in Irish, which one had to do to get the certificate. I do not forget that the principal of the day, the late Dr Irwin, retired on the same day that I left Wesley. Some would say that was not a coincidence. I'm sometimes asked, 'Well, what did Wesley do for you?' And my answer is: 'Its best.'

In 1945 I came to Enniskillen, where, in the interim, my father had bought the business which I was to go into and eventually run, until I retired about two years ago. Enniskillen is a lovely town; Fermanagh is a lovely county. Big enough, as I say, Enniskillen is, and has been, to allow one to pick and choose one's friends and yet small enough to allow one the opportunity of trying to make one's mark, as we say, in one's own town. Fifty per cent Protestant, near enough, and fifty per cent Roman Catholic. Although as a growing boy in Dublin I had heard of this Protestant/Catholic problem up north, it wasn't until I came to live in Enniskillen that I very quickly learned that, while there was one town, we had two distinct and very different communities, each with its own loyalty, its own heritage (to use a popular word), its own tradition. And there was this ongoing intolerance in the community. I do not forget that the first time the BBC *Songs of Praise* team came to Enniskillen, they asked me to choose a hymn and to say some words – and I'm talking about twenty-five or perhaps thirty years ago. I said then that, however lovely our town and however lovely our county, and however good our schools and hospitals, I was aware of an intolerance in our community which was unworthy of us. Looking back, it sounds almost prophetic. Things were being said in the community, at every level; by individuals, by groups, and of course at Stormont in Belfast, by *both* sides. And the communities were bouncing one off the other. It wasn't a problem for me; it never was and it never has been. I got on well with both communities. It suited me to get on well, to be honest, in that, if a man came in to me to buy a shirt, and I could establish a little of his trust in me and my trust in him, I could not care less which church he went to. But perhaps I was the exception.

I never got involved in politics, certainly not in party politics. Maybe I was frightened; maybe I just didn't have the guts for it. It seemed to be a hard world. And, of course, I was also conscious that the Protestants in my community, or in my town and county, might suspect me, just because I was from the

South, not perhaps a real Protestant in their eyes, and that the Roman Catholics might suspect me, just because I was a Protestant.

I'll tell a little story which, I think, very simply but clearly illustrates the sort of ongoing 'bouncing' that happened on a daily and nightly basis. We sold heavy underwear, lamb's wool underwear. The farmers bought it. It was made in Yorkshire and it carried a label, and on that label was a woven Union Jack, and I had decent Catholic farmers who wouldn't buy it. They saw it as waving the flag. Then the firm went out of business, and I found a firm in the County Dublin who made a similar sort of underwear, and the label on their garment said: 'Made in the Republic of Ireland'. I had decent Protestant farmers who wouldn't buy it. Now you may smile, you may even laugh, but, frankly, I didn't find that funny; I found that sad. But it is symptomatic of the sort of feelings and attitudes and approaches that people had on both sides.

I married my wife Joan in 1955. She is a local lassie from some six or seven miles out of town. Her father was a farmer. He lost a leg in the Great War, in France, and often talked about being sent home and nursed in Dublin by the nuns, and spoke very highly of them. Joan is a teacher, originally a primary school teacher, and then, for some fifteen or twenty years now, she has been teaching the violin. She is what is called a peripatetic teacher – that's the only five-syllable word I know! – in that she's not employed by any one school. She travels around. She is employed by the Music Service of the Western Education and Library Board.

We married in 1955, and got on with building up our home and family and, of course, for me life revolved around the business, and for Joan particularly, around our church, where she plays the organ and trains the choir. As a businessman, I got into the Chamber of Commerce and the Rotary Club. I played a little golf and a little tennis, and played bowls twice for Ireland. And life was good. We were comfortable.

We had three children: Peter and Julianne and Marie. And then, twenty-five years ago, came the Troubles. The 'bouncing' I've talked about became suspicion, and suspicion led to distrust, and distrust to fear, and fear to hatred, and hatred to confrontation, and confrontation to death. An eye for an eye, and a tooth for a tooth. But we, as I suspect every family does in Northern Ireland, always thought it would be somebody else's eye, or somebody else's tooth. And what about Marie, our Marie? Born in 1967, the youngest, the pet, maybe a little spoiled because of that. I like to think you will understand if I say she was special. People say: 'What will you longest remember about her?' The answer is always the same: her smile. She was a smiler. I don't think we have a single photograph of her where she isn't smiling. She was not an intellectual, but she got two good 'A' levels. Big strong lassie; never seemed to sit down; active, into games, into music through her mum; won a Duke of Edinburgh Gold award. She loved people. She wasn't outwardly religious, but her heart was in the right place. We like to think she had a happy childhood. She was not to know it, but she was to become a child of our times. She was politically and religiously aware. Young people in Northern Ireland cannot be otherwise. I do not forget one evening at tea – she would have been, perhaps, nine – and she said to me: 'Daddy, what's wrong with the Catholics?' It's a tight question. I hope I was able to answer it fairly and justly. Something she'd heard …

I'll tell a couple of little stories about her, which perhaps illustrate best the sort of lassie she was. One evening, at tea again, she would have been fourteen years of age. She said: 'Dad …' – she knew that I was the one to speak to in this situation, not her mum – 'Dad, there's a disco in the cathedral hall on Saturday night.' And I said, 'Oh-oh,' and she said, 'Dad, will you please wait till I ask the question before you give me an answer. All my friends are going, and the Dean is going to be at the door, and it'll be alright. Dad, can I go?' And I said no. And she left the table in very bad humour, and went up to her bedroom. We could hear her crying. I let her cry away for a couple or three minutes, and then I went up and I said, 'Marie, I've changed my mind. You may go. But,' I said, 'there's a condition. I'm coming with you and I'll stay at the door and I'll talk to the Dean.' And she said, 'Are you mad? Are you mad?' She didn't go.

Fifteen years of age, she said to me one day, 'Dad, I need a pound or two. One of my friends is sixteen and three or four of us are going downtown to celebrate her birthday. We're going to have our tea downtown.' And I gave her a fiver, and she said, 'Dad, it mightn't be enough.' 'What do you mean, "It mightn't be enough"?' I knew that it would be fish and chips. She said, 'Well, we thought of going on to the pictures.' 'What's on in the pictures?' I'm sure you think that I'm a hard man. She said, 'Dad, I don't know. We're just going to the pictures.' I said, 'Marie, if there's anything about it that doesn't look right, I want your promise not to go in.' She promised. Five-to-eight, the doorbell rang. I was alone at home. It was Marie – I had given her a second fiver – £10 for a night on the town for a fifteen-year-old. She said, 'Ah, there was something about it I didn't think was right.' 'Oh? Did your friends go?' 'Yes.' I remember thinking, it takes a lot of courage for a fifteen-year-old to say to her sixteen-year-old friends, 'I'm not going in,' and I said, 'Marie, you did well. I'm proud of you.' I gave her back the second fiver which she had given me. And she looked me between the two eyes and she said, 'Dad, the name of the game is trustworthiness.' From a fifteen-year-old? But that was Marie Wilson.

She went to train in the Royal Victoria Hospital in Belfast when she was eighteen. She'd always wanted to nurse. We knew from day one that she had made the right choice, that she was in the right profession, because we saw her every weekend and she was happy. She was very fortunate in the friends she made. She chose her friends wisely and well. She didn't, of course, tell us about her day-to-day nursing situation, but we knew she was content. We learned a little about it afterwards and, like most homes who've had their troubles, life for the Wilsons is very much a before and an after. Everything that comes up is related to, 'Was that before or was that after?' We had a letter, for example, from one of the male tutors who was having a class of student nurses. It was a class in psychiatric nursing. He was playing the part of a man deeply depressed who needed help. He was asking these young student nurses for their help and Marie volunteered one or two suggestions. And he said, no, no. Then she said, 'In that case, all I can offer you is my friendship.' That was Marie Wilson.

Some six weeks after the bomb, we had a letter from a lady called Marie McDonald, an auxiliary nurse in the Royal Victoria Hospital, that part of it that is known as the Royal Belfast Hospital for Sick Children, the last area of the Royal Victoria in which Marie worked. I'd like to read you a paragraph or two from her letter. She was not to know it then, but some three years ago, her brother, a Belfast taxi driver, was shot dead in the middle of the city of Belfast. Marie McDonald wrote:

> *I worked with Marie Wilson in the Royal Belfast Hospital for Sick Children during the last two weeks of her life, and I have never, in fifteen years as a nursing auxiliary, been so drawn to anyone. She was the most delightful girl, with all the qualities required by a good nurse. As the days passed, I was struck by her caring and her compassion, which she had in abundance. I once saw her eyes fill with tears while nursing a mentally handicapped child, and the gentle way she handled the sick babies was very moving.*
>
> *Her spontaneous friendliness was very infectious. She greeted everyone with that lovely smile and they responded in like manner. On the day she was leaving our ward, I spoke to her for the last time, and my words comfort me now. I'm so pleased I said them to her when she was*

alive, and not about her when she was dead.
[There's a lesson there too.] *I told her she had
the most beautiful disposition and that her mum
and dad could be very proud of her. I also said,
if ever I was ill, it would be lovely to be cared
for by her. As she left the ward, I wished her
good luck in the future. Three days later she was
dead.*

Having done two years' training of her three-year course, Marie
came home on the 7th of November, the day before
Remembrance Sunday, 1987 – six years ago; sometimes it
seems like sixty-six. And she volunteered to come with me the
following morning, as I had done for forty years, to the annual
Remembrance Day war memorial service. Suddenly, it wasn't
somebody else's eye, nor somebody else's tooth. We stood with
perhaps a hundred and fifty, two hundred civilian people. The
parade had not yet arrived; the army, the RUC, the UDR, the
British Legion, ex-service men. It was about a quarter to eleven.
And we were standing where I had always stood, with my
back to the wall of a disused school. We were not to know it,
but immediately behind us, on the other side of the wall, was
the bomb. And then the bomb ... Six of the seven people within
five feet of where we stood died in that bomb. So is it any
wonder I ask myself, 'Why am I here in Montrose tonight?'
The gable wall began to collapse and fall on top of us. I was
thrown forward – it seemed to me, in slow motion – on top of
the people who were standing in front of me. And I remember
thinking as I fell: All I need is a big one and it's goodbye. I
didn't get the big one.

Then the rumble of the wall falling stopped, and I found
myself under four to six feet of loose rubble, and then the
silence. The deathly silence. And then the shouting. And then
the screaming. This was raw, naked terror. I was on my face.
I was conscious that I had survived. My right arm had been
thrown out in the fall and, in so doing, I had dislocated my
shoulder. And then somebody took my right hand. 'Is that you,

Dad?' I couldn't believe it. It was Marie. I remember thinking, Thank God, Marie is safe. 'Are you alright, Marie?' and she said, 'Yes. Dad,' she said, 'let's get out of here.' I said, 'Marie, we can't get out of here. We're caught, we're pinned in, we've got air, we can breathe. They'll come, they'll come. Give them time. Are you alright?' 'Yes.' And then she screamed. That was the first warning I had that something was wrong. Three or four times I asked her was she alright, and all the while holding her hand. And each time she said, 'Yes.' But each time she screamed. I couldn't understand why, on the one hand, she was telling me she was alright, and on the other hand, she was screaming. And when I asked her for what would have been perhaps the fifth time, 'Marie, are you alright?' she said, 'Daddy, I love you very much.' That was her moment of truth; those were her last words.

She had to have known she was hurt. She had to have known she was at Calvary's edge. And what glorious words she used as she joined her Heavenly Father. Not words of anger, nor words of hatred, nor words of selfishness; words of love. And because of them, Marie Wilson was mourned by millions the world over. And because of them Chris de Burgh wrote a song in which he said,

> 'Her words did more to make us one
> than a hundred years of the bomb and the gun.'

And because of them, my greatest honour is to have been Marie Wilson's dad.

I was taken to hospital – a scene of chaos; organised chaos, but chaos nevertheless. A scene of anguish and shock and tears and grief and death. I was among the minor injured, put in a wheelchair, and then Joan arrived, and then Peter and Julianne. And of course the question on our lips was: 'Where's Marie?' She had been taken from the rubble. She had a cardiac arrest, we learned later, as she came through the vestibule in the hospital. She was very obviously critically injured, and she was taken straight to theatre, where she got twenty-four pints of blood. All the theatre staff knew was that they had a young female on the table who was, of course, not able to tell them who she was. We learned later that she suffered very severe injuries from the waist down, and that she had brain damage as well. It might seem a dreadful thing to say, but I thank God that she was taken, because I could not do what Mrs Noreen Hill has done, to nurse her husband through a coma for six years, including this night. I don't think I would have had the courage to do what she's doing. People sometimes say to me, 'You've great courage,' and I will very often say, 'If you want to see the face of courage, go and talk to Noreen Hill. There's the face of courage.'

And so, she died. And then Joan came down and told me. That really wasn't the hassle that perhaps Joan thought it might be, because, by now, I knew enough to know the news was not going to be good. And then they allowed me home, and I remember saying to my family as we drove home at about five o'clock, perhaps, on a cold November afternoon, 'Folks, it's never going to be the same again. But let us try to muster all the dignity we can and especially in the next two or three days, because they're going to be very difficult.' We went home to a dark house, and we made some tea, and then the doorbell, and then the phone, and then people, God love them, came and they were great, and but for them, we would not have come through. About nine o'clock, I went out for a breath of fresh air. I saw two men coming towards me, one of whom I knew, an Enniskillen man, a producer with BBC Radio Ulster, Charlie Warmington. He introduced me to a man called Mike Gaston, a BBC reporter, and Charlie said, 'Would you tell Mike the story of this morning, for BBC radio?' And because it was Charlie, I agreed. We emptied a room in our home and I told Mike the story of the morning in a matter of two or three minutes. And then he said, 'How do you feel about the guys who planted the bomb?' He hadn't warned me that he was going to ask the question. The answer to it was to prove my moment of truth, and I said, 'I bear them no ill will, I bear them no grudge. Dirty sort of talk is not going to bring Marie Wilson back to life. I should pray for those guys tonight, and every night, that God will forgive them.' And I did, and I do.

I didn't say those words because they were the nice words to use, or the words that perhaps I thought my friends would expect me to use. I said them because I meant them, and they came from my heart. I had been put on a plane of love by Marie's last words to me, and I got the grace from God to accept a little of His love, and so to say what I said. I didn't feel angry, and I didn't feel hatred, and I still don't. I take no personal credit whatever. I just thank God for the strength of His infinite love. People said, 'How could you?' 'The man's potty,' 'He was drugged,' 'He was in shock,' 'It was quite irrational.' But many, many more saw what I had said as forgiveness. And the response, by my standards – by any standards, perhaps – was enormous. Page One, Item One, on every bulletin and every newspaper, across the world. And we had an avalanche of letters, phone calls, flowers, books of condolences. It was happening to the other families as well. Silences. Vigils. And, above all, prayers. I was aware, and so was my wife Joan, of a level of prayer for us that was quite palpable. I truly would have to say I didn't believe, to that extent, in the power of prayer, and we were enormously supported and carried through our loss and our grief by it.

We buried our dead, and the ordinary life of the town stopped for a week. The trouble was that, it seemed to me, very early on, perhaps even on the day after the bomb, that I was being perceived as the Voice of Enniskillen, the voice, perhaps, even of Northern Ireland, a voice for hope, a voice for peace, a voice for reconciliation. My head said to me: Be careful! because I knew that I was neither physically nor mentally capable of being any of those things, and I could very quickly be out of my depth. But you just wouldn't believe the sort of things that happened. The local monsignor, Seán Cahill, my friend, planned a memorial mass in his church, on the Thursday night, four days after the bomb, to allow his people, as I saw it, to say, 'We're sorry.' I was moved to go, and I went. I took a little stick for going, I might as well be honest. But I was not to know that there would be three television cameras, and the cardinal, the late Cardinal Ó Fiaich, present, and that my presence at that service went out live on the RTÉ main 9 o'clock news, and on BBC network news that evening. That was the sort of pressure that I was coming under.

I was asked to do all sorts of things; for example, the BBC television crew wanted to come and live with the Wilsons for a week, and watch us eating and sleeping, and doing whatever, so that they could make a programme about the Wilsons to put out a year later, on Remembrance Sunday. We said 'no' to that one. I was asked to start a peace movement. I didn't do that. Somebody in America, a promoter, rang somebody he knew in Fermanagh, and said, 'Could you get this guy Wilson to tell his story in America or to come to America? Does he realise he's sitting on a million bucks?' I didn't do that one either.

The Lord Mayor of Dublin, Mrs Carmencita Hederman, came down with the books of condolence, which thousands and thousands of people queued in the rain to sign in Dublin, and of course in other cities as well. She had a prepared text, and she broke down in the middle of the first sentence, she was so moved by what had happened in Enniskillen. We had Prince Charles and Princess Di, eight days after the bomb. And the Queen mentioned Joan and me by name in her Christmas broadcast the following Christmas, some six weeks after the bomb; that never happened before. I received all sorts of awards, including the Tipperary Peace Award.

I never allowed it to go to my head. What taught me the strongest lesson was when BBC Radio Four's listeners voted me their Man of the Year – Britain's Man of the Year, would you believe, for 1988! When I learned later that second in the vote was Prince Charles and third was Mr Gorbachev, and realised what happened to them ... I had no problem keeping my feet on the ground.

The World Methodist Council presented me with their Peace Award in 1988, and on the night it was presented, in Enniskillen, I said: 'This is a peace award. What peace, you may well ask? Indeed, you might ask that poor woman who lost her daughter as well as her father in an explosion in Benburb only last week. In that sense of the word, there is no peace. Certainly not yet. But peace will come. Maybe not tomorrow, but come it will, because good must triumph over evil, and love will triumph over hatred. But,' I said, 'my peace is of another kind, and perhaps a better kind, because I enjoy the peace of knowing beyond doubt that Marie is in the presence of her Lord, and that, with God's will, we shall again hold her hand. I enjoy the peace of knowing that God is good, and my prayer is that he will be merciful to me, a sinner. I enjoy the peace of knowing that God is love, and that His grace is sufficient.'

Six weeks later, I lost my memory, and talked total rubbish for an afternoon and evening. I spent eight days in hospital, and the best medical brains in Northern Ireland could find nothing wrong, other than the fact that something had to give; it was to do with pressure, tension, and it was that part of the brain that affected the memory. Thankfully, it came back – at least I like to think it came back – the next morning.

The impact of Enniskillen was different. Hearts were touched, attitudes were changed and some good things came out of Enniskillen, and especially things to do with young people. Very quickly let me mention two, one of which, of course, is very close to our hearts, because it bears Marie's name, and is paid for by the Canadian government, where each year, under a scheme called 'The Marie Wilson Voyage of Hope', they bring some six or eight young people, equally divided from both communities, to a work camp in Canada, where they work, under the direction of nurses and doctors, with disadvantaged children. Apart from the value that they gain from that, they gain the value of meeting each other. These are all young Fermanagh people. And the other is the scheme called the Spirit of Enniskillen Bursary Scheme. On the day it was introduced, I said, 'The spirit of Enniskillen is the spirit of tolerance where there might have been retribution, of reconciliation where there might have been division, and of love where there might have been hatred.' For two years now, I have had the honour of serving on the panel which is chaired by the Chief Executive of Fermanagh District Council, a Mr Gerry Burns. We meet some lovely young people and we are now sending fifty of these young folk from all across Northern Ireland, again equally divided, in groups of ten, with a co-ordinator, to areas of the world where there has been, and maybe still is, a community problem, and they learn about it. But more importantly, they learn about each other, because the co-ordinator encourages them to talk about their situation, and their point of view, and their background, and their upbringing, and to listen to the others while they do the same. When I hear these young people come back and say they can never be the same young people again, and that they have seen the trip as really a total change in their thinking – not that we expect them all to agree with everything and with each other; that's not what we are asking of them. It opens their minds and it teaches them to listen, and to learn that there is another point of view which has to be respected.

Some two years ago, I retired. To be honest, after the bomb, I really didn't want to know about business. And then, with the help of a Belfast journalist called Alf McCreery, I wrote the Marie book. I knew it would mean getting my name back in the papers, but I felt there was a story to tell, and that it was worth telling. I felt it would be a fitting memorial to Marie, and I felt it would be a good therapy for myself. It was to prove to be all of those things.

And gradually one tries and has succeeded, to some degree, in coming to terms with life. I can be as public or as private as I want to be, or am able to be. I know I can never be the same man again. But I have not been led down the avenues of preaching, or getting involved with parties, or movements, or groups, and until seven or eight months ago – with politicians.

I don't see myself in the Senate in Dublin as a politician; I see it as a very great honour. I see it as an extension of a welcoming hand which I was happy to take. But that doesn't, in my book, make a politician out of me, because I am not a politician. I am happy to tell Marie's story, as I have tried to do this evening, if I am asked to do so. And through it all, my faith has been strengthened. John Greenleaf Whittier, the New England poet and hymn writer, puts it much better than I could ever possibly hope to, but I agree totally with what he says when he does say, in one of his hymns:

> I know not where his islands lift
> Their fronded palms in air
> I only know I cannot drift
> Beyond his love and care.

I am surer of God's love for me, and my need to love him, because only in his love can we have reconciliation and hope and peace. The bottom line is love. I have used the word over thirty times tonight, and I make no apology for doing so. Because I cannot believe that the mind of man who can send men to the moon and bring them back, with a little of the love of God in his heart, cannot find a solution for our lovely land, the Land of Saints and Scholars. Hopefully the document that was presented today [the Downing Street Declaration] is one giant step forward for Ireland. Hopefully, let us pray so.

I said I wasn't going to preach, but I'm going to finish with two or three verses of scripture, from the gospel of St Matthew, in chapter 22.

> An expert in the law tested him with this
>   question:
> 'Teacher, which is the greatest commandment
>   in the law?'
> And Jesus replied: 'Love the Lord your God,
>   with all your heart, and with all your
>   soul, and with all your mind.
> This is the first and greatest commandment.
> And the second is like it:

Love your neighbour as yourself.
All the law and the prophets hang on these
two commandments.'

So, if I accept those as the commandments of God, which I do, then I have to ask myself the question, 'Who is my neighbour?' And the answer I get is that my neighbour is not just the lady next door, and not just my Protestant neighbour, and not just my Catholic neighbour. Every man is my neighbour, and my neighbour must include my terrorist neighbour, because Christ died for them too.

1994

LEAVING THE PAST BEHIND

John Hume

*Civil Rights activist in Northern Ireland,
Member of Parliament since 1969,
co-founder and leader of the Social
Democratic and Labour Party,
member of the European Parliament,
one of the principal architects of the
Peace Process in Northern Ireland, for which he was
jointly awarded the Nobel Peace Prize, 1998*

John Hume

The past is something that we're very proud of in this island, and in that past there is much of which we can be proud. There's a lot in it that we cannot be proud of as well, because the past created our present, which isn't very pleasant. And if we continue with our respect for the past, it will paralyse our attitude to the future. One of the worst decades or periods of our past has been the last twenty-five years, when in the northern part of our island, three thousand one hundred and ninety human beings lost their lives. Of those, nine hundred and forty-five were members of the security forces; four hundred and twenty-eight of them were members of paramilitary organisations; eighteen hundred and seventeen of them were ordinary innocent civilians, like the people of Enniskillen, Greysteel, Loughinisland, and the Shankill. Eleven hundred and fifty-eight of them came from the Catholic community, and six hundred and fifty-nine of them came from the Protestant community. All sections of our community have suffered from our past failures to reach agreement among our people and provide the stability that this country is screaming out for. All those human beings who died are victims of our past failures.

In the city of Belfast, which has the highest churchgoing population in western Europe, on both sides of the religious divide, it has been necessary to build, not one, but thirteen walls, to separate and protect one section of the Christian people from another. Those walls are an indictment of all of us, because what they scream at us is that our past attitudes have built them. The positive way to look at them is as a challenge; if we want to bring them down and ensure that no future generation suffers from our failure to reach agreement, then the challenge is to re-examine our past attitudes, *all* of them. Given our commitment to past attitudes, particularly flag-waving attitudes, in this country, that is not going to be easy.

When you look at conflict, as it is my duty to do, in different parts of the world, looking for reasons and ideas, you find that conflict everywhere is really about the same thing; it's about seeing difference as a threat – the other side is a threat. It's about mindsets. We have those two mindsets in this island, and those two mindsets have to change. The Unionist mindset, for example, which is largely the Protestant tradition on this island, rightly and properly seeks to protect its identity and its heritage. That is an objective that every one of us should give a total commitment to, because every society is diverse and richer for its diversity, and respect for diversity is the basis of order in any society. The challenge to that mindset is not the Unionist objective, but the methods that they have traditionally used to achieve that objective of protecting their difference and their heritage. It is a simplistic mindset which exists in many parts of the world. I have described it as an Afrikaaner-style mindset – the way to protect themselves, given that they are in a minority on this island, is to hold all power in their own hands, and exclude everyone else. We who grew up in the North know what that leads to, as it would in any other society where that is done. It leads to widespread exclusion of a whole section of the community, whether that is based on colour or creed or nationality, and widespread discrimination, which, in the end, can only lead to conflict. The challenge to the Unionist mindset is to have the self-confidence in their own geography and in their own numbers, because this problem on this island cannot be solved without them and without their agreement. Victories are not solutions in divided societies. I look forward to the Unionist people and their leadership standing on their feet for the first time in our history and reaching agreement as to how we share this piece of earth. That is a challenge to the Unionist people.

Then there is the Nationalist mindset, largely drawn from the Catholic community on this island. Again, a traditionalist mindset which, in its own way, is a territorial mindset: this is our land and you Unionists are a minority; therefore you can't stop us uniting and running our own land. The challenge to that mindset is again simple, but profound: it is people who have rights, not territory. Without people, this piece of earth, however beautiful it is, this small island is only a jungle. When people are divided, by history and by loyalties, they cannot be brought together by any form of coercion. They can only be brought together by agreement. That applies to divided people anywhere. So agreement has to be our target and what we have to do is get all resources committed to promoting that agreement.

For the first time in our history, we now have the resources of both governments totally committed to 'encouraging, facilitating and enabling agreement among the people of this island'. The Downing Street Declaration defines the problem today, whatever about the past when there were selfish outside interests in the Irish situation. In the new Europe, today's problem is simply the divided people of this island. Therefore, if we really want to solve the problem, all resources ought to be devoted to promoting agreement. Whatever form the agreement takes, we work together and then the real healing process starts. In a generation or two a new Ireland will evolve, which will be built on agreement and on respect for differences. It will probably be very different from any of the traditional models that we've all been reared with as the ideal solutions. It's very easy to condemn Unionism for their past attitudes; it's very easy to condemn paramilitary organisations for what they have done, and vice versa. But as long as we do that, we preserve the past and we preserve the unpleasant present. We must draw a line over our past and recognise that everybody has been a victim of that past, or rather, a victim of the *failures* of that past to resolve our problems. We must draw a line over it, and let history judge it, look to the future, and face up to the major challenge of how do we reach agreement with one another on this small island.

Let us take example from other areas that have done this. Cast your mind back fifty years to the end of the Second World War. Thirty-five million people lay dead across this continent, for the second time in this century. For centuries, the peoples of Europe saw difference as a threat and slaughtered one another. Their answer to difference was to conquer those from whom they differed. Who could have forecast, fifty years ago, that representatives of the peoples of all those countries would be sitting in a European parliament, as part of a united Europe? And the Germans are still German, and the French are still French. Who could have forecast fifty years ago that we would have a united Europe today? It is the best example in the history of the world of conflict resolution. When you consider the awful bitterness between the European peoples, and the slaughter that it led to, and that now we're all together: how did they do it? That's a question that everybody in every area of conflict should ask. The answer, like all profundities in life, is simple: they decided that difference is not a threat; that difference is of the essence of humanity; that it's an accident of birth what you're born, and where you're born, and whether that accident of birth is colour, creed or nationality, it is not the choice of the person being born; it is the way we were born. So why should it ever be the source of hatred or conflict? There are not two human beings in the entire human race who are the same.

Difference is of the essence of humanity. Difference enriches humanity, and diversity enriches humanity. The peoples of Europe decided to respect their differences and to recognise that the divisions of centuries couldn't be healed in a week or a fortnight. They built institutions which respected their differences, which permitted them to work their common ground together, which is economics – bread on your table and a roof over your head; the right to existence, which is the most fundamental right, plus the right to a decent life. By spilling their sweat and not their blood, in building together, they broke down the barriers of centuries. The new Europe is gradually evolving, and it will continue to evolve.

I believe that that is what we have to do on this small island: respect our differences, build institutions which respect those differences, but which create the framework within which our healing process can take place, and within which we too can then work our very substantial common ground, which is economic. The first step on the road has been taken – a total cessation of violence – and it wasn't easy to get there. The decisions of the paramilitary organisations – who themselves are a product of our history –to lay down their arms will, I hope, prove to be historic decisions. The fact that we meet for the first time in a long time, in a peaceful atmosphere, should help us face up to that major challenge, because you do not heal the divisions of centuries, or the distrusts and prejudices of centuries, in a week or a fortnight. It is no longer the 1920s. When those military checkpoints leave our border, there will, in effect, be no border on this island. We are all part of a single market of Europe, with its free movement of goods, people and services. Once we start interacting together on the island for the first time in economic terms, some independent people have already forecasted that developing the trade among our island people could create up to 75,000 jobs. But the real border remains.

The real border is in the hearts and minds of our people. There are those who would tell us that partition is the problem of this country; it is not. What partition did was to institutionalise the real problem which was already there, and had been there for centuries. If Wolfe Tone wanted to unite the Irish people in 1798, they must have been divided. That division has been there for centuries. Partition simply institutionalised it and made it worse. The removal of the economic border leaves the real border in the hearts and minds of our people, and that's the challenge that we have to face up to in this new European world. We are living today in a post-nationalist world. There are those around Europe who still think that the nation state is something that is eternal. The nation state is only an era in history. Once upon a time, there were city states. Once upon a time we had high kings and we had kings, and then we had clan chieftains. The nation state has only been an evolutionary period in history, and when the history of the world is written, it will have proved to be one of the worst periods, because it caused not only imperialism, but two world wars.

Today's world is a much smaller world than in the 1920s, when the parents and grandparents of people in this room and people listening to me would hardly have left their own district in their lives. Today, you can sit in your own room and watch what's happening right across the world as it happens. There's no such thing as an independent country left in this world. We are interdependent. We cannot live apart. We are living in a post-nationalist world. The old traditional attitudes shouldn't harden our attitudes when we come to a table. We should recognise that the legacy of our past is still there, the divided people. But let us also work our common ground together, which is noncontroversial, and again I'm talking about economics.

We in this small island are the biggest wandering people in the world. In the last census in the United States of America, forty-two million people signed that they were of Irish extraction, from both our traditions. Most of their ancestry were driven from this island by famine, by injustice, by intolerance. Yet in today's world, they have come to the top – in politics, in government, in economics, in all fields. We have had presidents of the United States of Irish extraction, prime ministers of Canada, Australia and New Zealand of Irish extraction, and likewise leaders of the business communities in all those countries. The time has come to harness that, and to define Irishness today, not just simply those who live on the island, but let us harness the Irish *diaspora* as we tackle our economic problems, to use their influence across the world to market the products of our small industries on this island, and to seek the inward investment that will provide the basic right of existence to all our people. And doing that together, in both our traditions, using our links with both our traditions across the world, spilling our sweat and not our blood, will make a major contribution to the healing process and to the breaking down of barriers between our people.

In my own part of the world, we have already begun that process. The city of Derry was where the trouble started, and it was one of the worst examples of injustice in the old Northern Ireland. Today, we've put into practice the philosophy of respect for diversity. We alternate the mayor each year, from each section of the community, and chairmanships of committees of council go to all parties. Our differences are obvious, but the city is our common ground. And the community groups do the same on the ground. We have also been harnessing the Irish *diaspora*, taking small companies from right across the north of Ireland to America. We have got $45 million worth of orders from them in the last few years, and £120 million of inward investment. We can do that on a national basis, right across the country, north and south, playing both the Green and Orange cards positively for a change; for the positive benefit of this offshore island of the united states of Europe and of the United States of America. We are not asking them for charity, because we are offering them a foothold in the biggest single market in the world today – the European market – and we are offering them a quality of life which is going to be one of the major features in the new technological world that people will be seeking. If we harness ourselves in doing that, then we'll make a major contribution to the healing process in the main challenge, which is reaching agreement among our divided people. That agreement must, at least initially, create institutions, following the European model, which respect the diversity of our people, but allow us to work our common ground together.

Let us hope that this generation can face up to that challenge and leave our past behind us. And as we go into the next century, let us hope that it will be the first century in our island history when there will have been no killing of human beings on our streets, and no guns and bombs, and no emigration of our young. Let us hope that it will be an island in which Catholic, Protestant and Dissenter will truly live together in harmony and peace.

1995

THE UNITED NATIONS
IN THE REAL WORLD

SPEAKER

Erskine Childers

Former Senior Advisor to the United Nations
Director-General for Development and
International Economic Co-operation

Erskine Childers

Forty years ago, the first Irish delegation to the United Nations was in New York getting ready for Ireland's admission. What did we really join? Why has the UN's own fiftieth anniversary been clouded with so many problems? What sort of reform does the UN need for the challenges of today and tomorrow?

The best answers to these questions involve understanding that 'the UN' has two faces. One face is of the real world of all of us ordinary people, a UN that bespeaks the values of sharing and good neighbourliness, of reaching for the best in all human nature to build a truly just and gentle international society. The other face reflects the narrow little world of the power-elites of a few countries and their brutal premises of great-power politics, of might equalling right, of consigning the fate of the underprivileged and exploited to unaccountable 'market forces'.

Much of the story of the UN to date is a story of struggle between these contending forces for the soul, and the strength, or the arranged weakness, of our only universal public-service institution. This struggle has produced bizarre contrasts in the apparent performance of 'the UN', bewildering many citizens. In these remarks, I will try to outline the main features of the two faces of the UN, and recommend key remedial actions along the way.

The analysis I will offer may seem depressing, but I want to emphasise that from my own working experience and observation throughout the United Nations' system, and throughout the world, I know it can go on to even greater achievements if we can overcome the threats to it, because I know what it has already achieved. Let me at once mention only a few quick examples.

If the parliament of a single country with a homogeneous population of one culture had negotiated in 49 years the 70 detailed legal instruments that now make up our UN Bill of Human Rights, that parliament would be hailed for a truly historic accomplishment. In fact, between 51 and 180 governments in the UN General Assembly, representing every culture on Earth, have given us that Bill of Rights. Yet many politicians and journalists in Northern countries dismiss the same General Assembly as a mere 'talking shop'.

The idea of such international co-operation has, indeed, entered the collective mind of the international community, and when it decides to work together, the results are astonishing. In 1967, every nation joined under UN and World Health Organisation leadership in a sustained effort to rid the world of the age-old scourge of smallpox, which then afflicted 15 million people. Eradicating it required that every health service on Earth would follow a precise set of measures, day after day, without a single error. Only eleven years later, the 15 million cases had been reduced to none, anywhere on the planet.

As one other of numerous examples of such co-operation, for twenty years the UN Development Programme, with UNESCO – the UN's education agency – trained no less than 50,000 teachers a year, until over one million more teachers were at work than developing countries could have hoped for without the UN.

I could devote this entire lecture merely to reciting only the major achievements of the UN. But there is its other 'face', and because of it, the UN is today under active threat of extinction. We need to see how these two faces struggle for its soul, in order to know how to defend and to improve it.

The first face expresses all the most noble aspirations assembled from the human experience over thousands of years, and it makes much of the Charter read like an ideal constitution for the world. Listen for a moment to some excerpted passages:

... to reaffirm faith [in] the equal rights of men
and women and of nations large and small ... to
employ international machinery for the promotion
of the economic and social advancement of all
peoples ... encouraging respect for human rights
and for fundamental freedoms for all without
distinction as to race, sex, language, or religion
... [and] to be a centre for harmonising the actions
of nations in the attainment of these common ends.

The Charter's first Principle is: 'the sovereign equality of all
its Members'. This requires of the economically and militarily
powerful members that they accept and respect little Ireland's
vote in the General Assembly as always having equal standing
with theirs. This principle of 'one nation, one vote' is by no
means perfect: Ireland with 3.5 million people has the same
one vote as India with 900 million people Yet, uncannily, the
one-nation–one-vote formula does provide an overall
framework for equitable decision-making between the weak
and the powerful. For the proportion of all votes that is held
by the better-off minority in the North very closely equates
with their share of the world's population; and the percentage
of votes held by the majority of humankind, the poorer
developing countries, almost exactly matches their proportion
of the world's population. We will have to rest content with
this admittedly rough planetary democracy until the mistrust
generated in the majority by the constant attempts of the
minority to control the UN can be removed by a new spirit
and good-faith co-operation.

It is important to probe a little deeper between the two faces
of the UN on this issue. China and India have one-third of the
whole world's population between them, but neither has ever
expressed dissatisfaction that they each have only one vote
alongside that of tiny countries. In the United States, however,
although it unreservedly accepted one nation, one vote in
signing the Charter, today leaders of the US Congress demand
weighted voting throughout the UN.

They do not question Ireland's, or say Luxembourg's, one vote alongside theirs; it is the votes wielded by coloured hands from non-Western cultures that they do not find comfortable. They offer all sorts of arguments to defend this; for example, that many developing countries are not democratically governed. This very conveniently evades the major responsibility of the Western powers for the dictatorships their intelligence agencies installed, financed and armed in country after developing country during the Cold War. Moreover, the developing country that has most consistently annoyed the major Western powers has been India, a functioning parliamentary democracy.

The real problem is that these power elites have not yet shaken off the deeply ingrained subconscious notion that the white Christian North is somehow destined to rule the world. Politicians, educators, spiritual leaders and non-governmental organisations must give this apartheid of the mind far more serious attention, lest it contribute to a global convulsion.

All members are also bound in international law to respect the freedom of the equal vote of each member, regardless of size or strength. However, both in the Security Council and in the General Assembly, whenever one or more of the powers wants to prevent a resolution being adopted by the majority of nations of the world, or wants to railroad through a resolution, they inform poorer and weaker members that if they do not vote the right way, they will lose all 'aid', not get debt relief, or lose their international credit standing through the International Monetary Fund.

Obviously, if this practice continues, more and more countries will cease to think membership in the UN is worth the brutality meted out to them by being members. To avert such gradual collapse we must mount a 'Blackmail Watch' at the UN, and raise a Blackmail Defence Fund, so that any threatened member will know that, if it refuses to surrender its freedom of vote, fellow-members will help it through the economic damage the powers may inflict upon it.

Linked with the UN's democratic principles are those laid down for financing the UN. The Charter says that 'the expenses of the organisation shall be borne by the Members as apportioned by the General Assembly'; and right from the beginning, the formula for such apportionment agreed by everyone – again, including the United States – was relative capacity to pay. This is based on the principles of taxation in every democratic country.

Seen in Irish terms, this means that it is as great a burden for the Irish citizen with a low income to find his or her small amount of tax each year for the Irish exchequer as it is for the wealthier Irish citizen or corporation to find a larger money amount of tax. In democracies, this equalising of tax burden is a foundation of the further principle that richer citizens or corporations should not have any special representation or voting strength in parliament, or positions in governments.

The same principles are the very foundations of financing the UN. The amount Ireland contributes as its dues is calculated from the same democratic principle of equality of burden. Ireland pays much less in its dues in money amount than, say, Germany; but the burden of finding her smaller share is just as great as Germany's in finding her larger amount. Accordingly, no member state is supposed to have any special influence in the UN organs except in the Security Council, which we will come to presently.

These democratic principles are, however, now under constant challenge, not only by the United States, but by other Northern industrial countries. In complete violation of Charter principles, they claim that since they contribute 'most' in money amounts to the UN's budgets, they should have a special, predominant say in all UN policies. If we are to re-establish a basis of North-South trust, every government must reaffirm the UN principle of equity of burden – that in the United Nations, everyone 'pays most'.

Worse again, however, early in the 1980s, the United States began withholding its legally assessed dues to force the membership to accept, among other demands, budgeting by consensus, despite the Charter provision that the budget is approved by a two-thirds majority of the General Assembly. Weakened by their deeper impoverishment and rising indebtedness, the majority accepted budget approval based on 'the broadest possible agreement', provided the United States would resume paying its full dues. Ten years later, however, the United States is still not paying its full dues.

As a direct result, the UN is now on the very brink of outright bankruptcy. It is owed over 2 billion dollars. Most West European countries, including Ireland, pay in their regular and peacekeeping dues promptly. The very host country to the UN – the United States – owes over a billion dollars, not because the US cannot afford to pay, but because it refuses to unless every other member accepts whatever unilateral demands it makes to change UN policies. Other countries, principally Russia and the Ukraine, are in deep arrears, especially on their peacekeeping contributions, but for economic reasons, not political blackmail. The developing countries' share of the arrears is only 12 per cent.

The United States' apportioned share of UN budgets – 25 per cent of the regular budget, 32 per cent of peacekeeping – is actually less than a strict application of the burden-sharing formula would require. But all accumulated experience indicates that it is simply not safe to have the UN so dependent on, and so liable to political ransom by, any one country. All other governments, and their citizens' organisations, must now energetically campaign for a revision of the assessment scheme, so that the United States (or any other country in the future) pays no more than 10 or 12 per cent of a UN budget. The difference in the reduced US assessment must be reapportioned among other financially capable countries. The new assessment rate should apply to the US on the day when it pays in all its arrears.

A third feature of the noble face of the UN involves another almost uncanny legacy from the founders – in the scope and the major emphasis of the Charter that they adopted in 1945. The world around them was a world of empires, with much of humankind imprisoned and exploited inside them. Few could imagine that political structure of the world significantly changing at any time in the 20th century. Belgium, Britain, France, the Netherlands, Portugal and the Soviet Union were all busily retrieving imperial possessions seized by the Axis Powers, or maintaining those that had not been. So distant did the prospects seem for independence for all the peoples locked up inside the empires that the architects of the new UN headquarters at New York were told to make plans for an expansion of the membership from 51 to only 'about 70'. And most of the 20 more members envisaged were going to come from Europe, including Ireland whenever the Soviet Union stopped vetoing our admission because of our neutrality in the Second World War.

If you visit the UN at New York, you can still see the effect of these original assumptions in the organisation of the flags of the members. Flagpoles for the world, as it was assumed it would be far into the future, were all to be displayed in front of the UN buildings, with enough space for another 20 or so. Today, the flags of 185 members have to extend far away among the trees of the UN gardens, judiciously rotated by alphabetical order, so that everyone's national colours get their turn to be better seen.

As Ireland's flag was added in December 1955, this overturning of the assumptions of 1945 was just beginning. The whole timetable of releasing most of humankind from the comprehensive prison of colonialism had suddenly accelerated by decades.

Inspired by the UN's Charter and Universal Declaration of Human Rights, national liberation movements were rebelling all across the South like a racing grass fire. Ireland was joining a UN that was about to be totally transformed by the admission of dozens of countries altogether outside of Western, Judeo-Christian culture.

It would not have been surprising if a Charter written in 1945 had proven inadequate for this enormous trans-formation. Yet, almost as if some unseen, but farseeing hand had guided its drafters, most of the principles and work-programme in the Charter provided a remarkably sound framework to tackle the whole world's problems, as decolonisation made the UN nearly universal by the early 1970s. In a very real sense, the founders had written the first-ever social contract for humankind, only waiting to come into its own when all of humankind would be free.

The smaller nations that could be at San Francisco, and the best thinkers from the larger ones, had been intensely aware that upheaval and conflict anywhere have their roots in cultural, political, economic and social conditions. If succeeding generations were to be saved from 'the scourge of war', then the causes of war must be comprehensively addressed, especially the economic and social causes, including deprivations of fundamental human rights.

The smaller nations managed to balance the great powers' emphasis on enforcing peace through the Security Council, with an Economic and Social Council that is expressly charged with tackling the causes of threats to peace. And they managed to have the Charter clearly mandate the UN to be the leader in economic and social policy for all people, to build lasting foundations for a peaceful and equitable world.

Enter again the other face of the UN. Ever since decolonisation gave the majority of humankind its majority in the UN, the elites of the industrial powers have not been willing to allow the UN to exercise the global economic leadership which its founders intended. Although without any legal grounds, they say that the International Monetary Fund (IMF) and the World Bank are mandated to deal with global macroeconomic issues, and that they will therefore not participate substantively in any such discussion in the Economic and Social Council or the General Assembly. But they do not allow the IMF and World Bank – which they control – to deal with these issues either.

The United Nations is thus disenfranchised from the real economy of all humankind. The industrial powers have, to be sure, helped to finance the UN's development assistance programmes, but they have never to this day been willing to address the real problems which even far larger development 'aid' could not possibly solve – the denial of fair trading opportunities to the developing countries to enable them to earn their way in the world.

As a result, one in every four of us alive on Earth this day is sunk in absolute poverty. The gap between the North and South has doubled since 1960; then, the poorest one-fifth of humankind was at least earning one-thirtieth what the richest one-fifth in the North was earning; today they cannot even earn one-sixtieth what people in the North earn. And the paramount reason can be summarised in one other appalling statistic: 80 per cent of humankind now have only 19 per cent of world trade.

But the hectoring preachers of the market religion insist that governments can do nothing effective about this; and what is more, they should not even try, because only 'market forces' decide who prospers. The 'miracles' their advocates hold up to the world may recurringly blow up in their faces, as in Mexico the other day, hurtling more millions into poverty. One electronic speculator may earn over a billion dollars in personal profit in 36 hours of manipulating a whole portion of a nation's currency reserve back and forth across the world. No matter and never mind; these are the mysterious forces of the market which governments must leave alone, and which the United Nations must not even discuss. It is rubbish, but it is toxic, dangerous rubbish.

These two faces of the UN are vividly evident in a comparison between the two major branches of the UN's mandated work.

On one hand, the Economic and Social Council is supposed to tackle the socioeconomic causes of upheaval and conflict; but, rendered impotent by the refusal of the industrial powers to discuss macro-policy at the UN, it meets for only 5 weeks in the year. On the other hand, the Security Council, which was supposed to have as little work as possible, meets in continuous session in face of over 60 active armed conflicts that have erupted across our world because no one addressed their causes in time.

There is therefore no more urgent challenge on this planet than to redeem this dangerous imbalance. The UN's economic and social machinery must be urgently re-invigorated and programmed to tackle the causes of the conflicts that are erupting from all the neglected legacies of empire and cold war, exacerbated by the economic policies of the industrial powers. We need a carefully articulated sequence of negotiations throughout the UN system, leading to a single comprehensive UN Conference on Money, Trade, Finance and Sustainable Development. That Conference should do two things: adopt all-win strategies to eliminate world poverty, and adopt reforms of the UN system to enable it to mount a more effective, properly co-ordinated attack on world poverty.

These reforms should include bringing the IMF and the new World Trade Organisation fully into the UN system and under the direction of the General Assembly. Every government should be fully aware of what is at stake in the present chaotic lack of co-ordination. To give one quick illustration: because the IMF is allowed by the powers to operate on its own, it has imposed so-called 'structural adjustment' programmes on over 90 developing counties, including ordering them to slash the educational services they painfully built up with UN help; so in many countries over 30 per cent of those teachers who were trained with UN help between 1965 and 1985 have been fired.

We have got to end this nonsense and make the UN system a real system, if we are at last to tackle the causes of upheaval and conflict, and avert a relentless coalescing of currently escalating tensions into one global North-South conflict. The members of the European Union hold these vital keys to world peace in their own hands, because the elites in industrial powers will not listen to anyone else.

But there is still the most ugly feature of the other face of the UN, the veto power of the five self-named Permanent Members. Because of this, the Charter suddenly reads in various places like a beautiful democratic constitution abruptly amended by a fascist coup d'état. China has indicated extreme reluctance to use its veto power, and Russia is heavily preoccupied with its post-Soviet internal problems. Three countries really make up this unseemly club – Britain, France and the United States.

Although lecturing the rest of the world, day in, day out, to practise democracy, they have never submitted themselves for election to the Security Council in 50 years. Like the paramount barons of a feudal council 500 years ago, the 'Permanent Members' are there 'as of right' – right defined by themselves. In addition to being able to veto new admissions (like Ireland's for a decade), they gave themselves veto power over nominations to the post of chief public servant of the world, the Secretary-General; veto power over UN initiatives to settle disputes peacefully; veto power over UN peace enforcement; and to complete these blights in the Charter, they can veto any amendment to it that might end these self-arrogated powers.

The 'Permanent Members' gave as their reason for demanding these special privileges that they were the major military and economic powers in the world, and would bear the special responsibility of being the world's policemen. For the next 40 years, far from policing the world, four of them bankrupted themselves, and diverted vast sums that could have been used for the advancement of most of humankind in stockpiling enough nuclear weapons to kill every child, woman and man on the planet ten times over. At the end of this insanity in 1990, they again promised that they would be the policemen of 'a new world order'. But except for a Gulf War to protect oil prices and profits, and to smash Iraq for special reasons of *realpolitik*, they have not agreed on, or contributed, adequate resources for preventing any of the armed conflicts that have raged across the planet since the Cold War's constraints ended. And they are now more and more openly saying that they cannot afford to be, and their citizens do not wish them to be, the policemen of the world.

Well and good, but we need to realise all of what this means for the UN.

The difficulties of the UN's Peace Missions in a variety of crises – former Yugoslavia, Somalia, Rwanda, for example – have originated with these Permanent Members. In every single case, they refused to approve the size of UN force that was recommended by the Secretary-General; they authorised only a smaller force with a totally inadequate and ambiguous mandate, and denied the vital logistical and other resources that even that inadequate force needed. In addition, one or more of these powers has intervened unilaterally in crises in which the UN has already been committed.

The UN's resultant difficulties are then neatly transformed into – and I quote the standard phraseology – 'another UN fiasco'. In the United States, the deaths of US Rangers who made a raid into Mogadishu in Somalia without the UN Force there even being told they were coming are now being called a 'UN fiasco'.

Member-governments must cease their shameful silences over this repeated cynical unloading of great-power mistakes onto the good name of the United Nations – and the memory of the men and women who have died in its service. Use of the UN as a scapegoat for great-power incompetence must be stopped in its tracks, lest it destroy the credibility of the UN before its member-peoples.

The very recent decision to insert a NATO force into former Yugoslavia changes nothing about the overall prospects for United Nations peacekeeping under the present Security Council. Having waited until 250,000 people have died and 2.8 million have been displaced from their homes, the powers have now mounted a force larger and with a stronger mandate than they were willing to authorise under the UN at the very time when the conflict might have been contained and so much misery and brutality averted. And naked domestic politics have driven even this decision.

The lessons must be seen very clearly. First, the Security Council under control of the Permanent Members is quite simply dishonest with the international community; it repeatedly falsifies the very analysis of what a crisis calls for. Secondly, it has ceased to be responsible; it sends out palpably under-resourced and under-mandated Peace Missions that are bound to run into trouble. Thirdly, even when they are not willing to contribute their due share of a peacekeeping operation, one or more Permanent Members use the threat of veto to keep the rest of the UN community from acting without them.

The Permanent Members are thus not only declining to be the policemen of the world they have twice said they would be; they will not allow the rest of the world even to try to police itself without them.

Bearing all of the foregoing factors in mind, we face some drastic decisions. We must recognise that the Security Council as currently constituted is no longer a trustworthy organ for UN peacekeeping. It will not become trustworthy by merely expanding the Permanent Member club, inviting in more emperors without clothes, extending this feudal anomaly in the UN into the 21st century.

This Security Council is not reformable so long as the Permanent Members can veto an end to their own status. It must, therefore, be bypassed. The General Assembly has the power to render it inert simply by ceasing to elect its ten non-permanent members, leaving the five, four, three, two, one in splendid isolation until their citizens insist on joining the real world. The General Assembly must be prepared to assume the UN's peacekeeping responsibilities through a smaller subsidiary of itself created for these purposes under Article 22 of the Charter.

Secondly, since Permanent Members cannot be counted upon to play their proportionate part, the rest of the UN membership must regroup and reorganise to respond to crises that will continue to erupt until we successfully redress their causes.

Far more reliance should be placed upon regional bodies like the Organisation of African Unity, helping them to develop early-warning, mediation, and peacekeeping capacities. Ireland should also join with other ordinary countries with veteran peacekeeping experience to identify what greater flexibility of response is needed to reduce the need for and the higher costs of full-scale military deployments – for example, a stand-by volunteer UN Humanitarian Security Police Force. Logistical resources need to be more ready, and even pre-positioned, for countries that can contribute troops but lack the equipment.

Finally, we must improve United Nations leadership, at the top and from the base. For the world ahead, we will need a strong, courageous Secretary-General who can mobilise the confidence and support of the peoples of the United Nations; I believe we need an outstanding woman next time. And from the base, we must work to establish alongside the General Assembly of executive government a United Nations Parliamentary Assembly elected by the member-peoples. That is not so wild as it may at first seem – only the equivalent of reproducing some seven Indian democratic elections. It is time for 'we, the peoples of the United Nations' to be more involved in its work than merely having the opening lines of the Charter and never being heard again.

The recommendations I have made in this analysis may seem 'unrealistic', until it is realised that they all involve overcoming one paramount problem. That is the profound psychological programming of our minds, by imperial history and by today's cynicism, to be obeisant to so-called 'great powers'. It is a programming that commensurately undervalues ourselves, all of us ordinary peoples around the world who have no overweening pretensions. It is an extremely dangerous and invariably damaging subservience to a myth.

At last, those who have maintained the myth are themselves evincing signs of weariness, of hopelessly wrong diplomatic analysis and decision-making; and their present additional trance to the magic of the market will not last much longer either. But we cannot afford to wait for them, poor tired relics of the imperial age, to abandon their pretences – or even for their own citizens to put them out to pasture.

The United Nations is an idea and an ideal for the real world and for real people, not pathetic little elites in a few countries who traduce not only us but their own decent citizens. They have so neglected the real causes of conflict and have for so long denied the United Nations its paramount role in resolving those causes, that the post-Cold War world is now like a gigantic minefield. We have got to act together to re-empower our United Nations urgently, if we wish to leave a more just and gentle world to our children.

We can save the UN and we can make it work for the kind of world all our children everywhere will need. Ireland is only one small player in this challenge, but teamed up with all the other players, Ireland becomes more than ourselves.

That is precisely what was best in the meaning of the Charter we were all given fifty years ago. We must now renew it, together, while time remains.

1996

THEME

OPEN BOOK, OPEN MIND
(WHY WE READ BOOKS
AND WHY WE NEED THEM)

SPEAKER

Anne Fine

*Award-winning author of
children's and adult fiction*

Anne Fine

It seems a prodigious nerve to come to Dublin and presume to talk to the Irish about the value of books and reading. My only excuse is that you were kind enough to invite me, and that you were kind enough to come tonight to listen to me, and thank you very much for that. The title for my talk this evening is 'Open Book, Open Mind', but I really do feel that I could have expanded it even further to 'Open Heart and Open Soul', because what I want to talk about tonight is the way in which books are, without a doubt, the best and most pleasurable medium that we have for self-development and self-enrichment, and how, because of this, the more books that are opened, and the more books read, the better things will be for all of us individually and, by extension, for society in general.

I confess, at the start, that I am presenting you with no formal argument here. One of the few things that I am sure about myself is that I have no scholar's mind. What I was born with, and all I still have, after all my teachers' efforts, is what we might call the 'jackdaw' mind of the imaginative writer. It's a somewhat 'grab-bag' affair. I am not alone in this, among writers. Patrick White described his own mind once as:

> ... more like the calico bag hanging from the sewing room doorknob, stuffed with snippets of material of contrasting textures and clashing colours which might, at some future date, be put to some practical, aesthetic or even poetic use.

This talk, I have to warn you, is full of snippets, and what authority I claim comes largely from minds that work a lot better than mine. But the use to which I am going to put my slightly patchy offerings is a paean of praise for literature, a plea for more reading of fiction, for 'Open Book, Open Mind' is not, for me, just a title. It's actually a credo as well. This I believe. And it is with this belief firmly in mind that I have spent my working life. Sometimes, I fear, I am as committed and obsessed on this subject as Mr Wimbush in Aldous Huxley's novel *Crome Yellow,* and secretly share the views that he confided when one of the other characters in the novel asks him:

> 'Well, what about the desirable human contacts – like love and friendship?'
>
> Mr Wimbush shook his head. 'The pleasures even of these contacts are much exaggerated. It seems to me doubtful whether they are equal to the pleasures of private reading and contemplation. Human contacts have been so highly valued in the past only because reading was not a common accomplishment, and because books were scarce and difficult to reproduce. The world, you must remember, is only just becoming literate. As reading becomes more and more habitual and widespread, an ever increasing number of people will discover that books will give them all the pleasures of social life and none of its intolerable tedium. At present, people in search of pleasure naturally tend to congregate in large herds and make noise. In future their natural tendency will be to seek solitude and quiet. The proper study of mankind is books.'

And Mr Wimbush, committed as he is, has not even mentioned the visionary side of reading for pleasure. In her autobiography, *To the Island,* Janet Frame describes how her early reading as a child coloured what was obviously otherwise a strained world.

> There was no removal of myself and my life to another world. There was simply the other world's arrival in my world – the literature

streaming through it like an array of beautiful
ribbons through the branches of a green growing
tree, touching the leaves with unexpected light.

And neither, I have to say, did Mr Wimbush mention how
books can bring you to yourself. In *Of Human Bondage*, one
of Somerset Maugham's characters is asked the most basic
question: 'Why do you read, then?' and his answer is, I think,
a telling one:

> 'Partly for pleasure, because it's a habit and I'm
> just as uncomfortable if I don't read as if I don't
> smoke, and partly to know myself. When I read
> a book, every now and then I come across a
> passage, perhaps only a phrase, which has a
> meaning for me and it becomes part of me. You
> see, one's like a closed bud but there are certain
> things that have a peculiar significance for one
> and they open a petal and the petals open one by
> one and at last the flower is there.'

Now, some of you, I suspect, on hearing these descriptions of
how reading works, will be nodding along inwardly with me,
and others – presented with such high-flown imagery of petals
unfurling into full flower and the like – will find yourselves
recoiling somewhat, and I, as a writer, have some sympathy
with this. We, of all people, I think, have reasons to be wary
about moralising about the purpose of a book. In a novel, *A
Private Place*, Amanda Craig has a librarian with whom a lot
of us have a good deal of sympathy. He claims that art is like
love, and has no point.

> 'Of course,' he says, 'people are always trying
> to give it a moral value, claiming that it ennobles
> or informs. That's nonsense, in my opinion. It
> may do both those things, incidentally, as a sort
> of by-product, but really art and love are about
> the same utterly useless thing.'
> 'What's that?'
> 'Enchantment,' said the librarian.

And he is right, to the extent that the justification for any piece of fiction must, in the last analysis, be that it is a good read. Stuck in a lift with a writer on the way home from an event like this, your safest remark for starters will always be: 'I'm sorry, call me a madman if you will, but I could not put your book down.'

The writer's first job is to grab you by the lapels, to keep you reading, and to keep you turning the page. We consider it a major triumph if you miss your bus-stop. We are prouder than any toddler to keep you up until two in the morning. If we have a sliver of ice in the heart, this is what it is about, because if you put down the book, we've failed, whether you're six or sixty, and at the back of our minds, we always hear Will Cuppy's famous remark about a library book that he'd clearly ploughed to page forty or so, and then clapped shut. He said: 'It was *unreadable*. And, for me, that always sort of spoils a book.' So it's nice if the book has added value. In my novel *Goggle Eyes*, Kitty's teacher says what many believe:

> Living your life is a long and doggy business,
> and stories and books help. Some help you with
> the living itself, some help you just take a break,
> and the best do both at the same time.

But if you can't read them, they can't be the best, whatever the clever critics say and we all know it. You can read Thackeray. You can read Flaubert and Tolstoy and Austen and George Eliot. You don't get lost halfway through an Anthony Trollope. You don't wonder where you are halfway through *Middlemarch*. So, first, readability, and then sheer fearless honesty on the part of the author. As Joseph Conrad says: 'The artist's duty is to make you *see*.' And here's where a petal or two will start opening, I can assure you, because facing a frank and honest portrayal of human emotion is probably the best way of coming to some sort of understanding of it. It's fiction's job to hold the mirror up to life, to take the individual case, usually a totally invented individual case, and use it to illuminate the general. And this very individuality can give the reader both insight and hope. No one is, after all, simply part of a statistic and nothing more. In the film *Shadowlands*, a young man reports his teacher father as saying: 'We read to know that we are not alone.' And it is true. In a good book, the reader gets to know the characters better than they may ever get to know even their own friends and families. It's not by accident that Graham Swift, accepting his Booker Prize, thanked his readers so warmly and unreservedly. After all, these people had, as he pointed out, taken him into their beds, into their baths, and you don't get much more intimate than that. And the author repays this intimacy in kind – in spades, some would say – by offering something even more intimate in return: the truth. Everybody is agreed on that.

Here's Picasso: 'Art is a lie that tells the truth.'

Here's Clive James: 'Good art compresses the coal of truth into diamonds.'

Here's Alan Massey, speaking through one of his narrators: 'A novel must carry an inward truth that goes much deeper than appearances, that can take wing beyond the particular. Novels are true or they are nothing.'

And here is Martin Amis, whose books so many people have found so disturbing, raising the writer's unassailable defence: 'It's not *your* truth, but it's *my* truth, and it's part of *the* truth.'

Because books can be disturbing, disquieting. They raise the question: how ought we to live? They are a moral template for us all. *Would I have been that cowardly or that brave? That mealy-mouthed or that frank? That feckless or that steadfast?* Books show us not just the world, but ourselves as well. And self-scrutiny is an underrated virtue. I think lack of self-knowledge is at the root of an unacknowledged amount of misery in people's family lives and all around us. Books can, and do, make people stop and think. Kafka said: 'Art should serve as the axe for the frozen sea within us,' and we all come across so many people into whose hands we itch to thrust a particular book. 'Here – read this. You'll think and feel differently afterwards.'

And it does *have* to be a book. Television and film just won't do. Books can explore emotion. They can be reflective, they can expose conscience and motivation, morals and inner concerns. They do not simply show you what happened next at the producer's speed; they show you how and why, at your own. For it is the job of the writer to be articulate, to make with the words about even the deepest and most private matters, to explain exactly why this man poisoned his mother; that woman left her husband; and this child kissed the frog. Ford Madox Ford once wrote that imaginative literature was the most important thing in the world, because it is the only thing that can make you think and feel simultaneously. I doubt if there's anybody here who really believes the world couldn't do with a little bit more reflectiveness. We see so many around us – young and old – who seem to have brought down the shutters on sympathy and on imaginative empathy. And it is hard to believe that they haven't, at some point along the road, been forced – maybe in some macabre form of self-protection – to harden their hearts and souls against feeling, until they actually do become seemingly unfeeling themselves. We can dish out words like 'childhood neglect'. We can worry about the unassimilable violent images with which so many of us feel ourselves bombarded. But there can't be that many of us who don't feel that, however the problem has arisen, to be around people who are entirely impoverished in their understanding of how they themselves, and other people, tick, is as frustrating as being, for example, an engineer living among people who have never understood the most basic scientific principles – of the lever, say, or the pump. Though he was speaking of the value of poetry, Norman McCaig put it best:

> What use is it? It trains, educates, extends the
> range of our sensibility, as science and technology
> train the intellect. That is to say, the arts induce

us to respond to, and examine, the emotional significance as well as the rational significance, of whatever comes under our notice, and to have unexamined emotional responses is as much a sign of immaturity as to have unexamined beliefs. Now, an adult physique with the intelligence of a child is looked after. It might some day put an axe in someone's skull. An adult intelligence with the emotional equipment of a child is just as dangerous, maybe more.

And books are not just an enlightenment; they are a comfort too. I mean, there cannot be an adult in this room who has not put down a book with a sigh of recognition, a sense of '*Yes! That is exactly how I feel! That is exactly how things are for me*' – a sense of no longer being on one's own. In some cases, even more liberating, '*So I'm not the only woman to feel this way! I'm not mad, or at least no madder than all the rest.*' Many of us, I think, remember the particular book that let us out of the particular box. 'Literary experience,' CS Lewis said, 'heals the wound without undermining the privilege of individuality. In reading I become a thousand men, and yet remain myself.'

We adults find it comforting enough. Think what this avenue of vicarious experience can mean to younger readers. As people like the Opies have shown, children have always learned necessary skills and virtues from the stories offered them. In the past, from the old tales told around the fire, they learned the value of courage, endurance, quick wits, courtesy to strangers (however ugly) at the well. 'Drop the pebbles from your pocket when the wicked stepmother takes you into the wood; don't panic – wait for the moon to come up before you try to find your way home.' Children today can't get lost in forests, unless they are total halfwits. Within two minutes, they'd have found the car park or the information centre, or one of those little arrowed posts, and we no longer encourage them to talk to strangers at all. But they do need to learn other things from books. So, what is a writer like me doing in a book like *Madame Doubtfire*? or *Book of the Banshee*? or *Flour Babies*? After all, I don't expect my readers to identify particularly with any of my characters. They'll be the wrong age, or the wrong sex, or the wrong temperament, or '*My dad's not like that*,' or '*We're not that rich*.' But, in a comedy like *Madame Doubtfire*, under, between and inside the jokes, I'm trying to show them that it's difficult to be the mother in this family. It's difficult to be the father. It's difficult to be Lydia and Christopher and little Natalie. And in the length of the book, the reader gets to see how everyone feels – not something you would ever learn from the film.

And the reader watches them survive: still cracking jokes, still trying by their lights, however dim.

It is tolerance and understanding that liberate our children now. They are the 20th century equivalents of the pebbles gleaming in the moonlight and showing the way out of the forest. I believe that a child who cannot even bear to begin to think about his or her own situation can often begin, quite safely, to explore the problems they face, and the feelings they have, through fiction – someone else's problem, someone else's feelings. And even those of us who think our children are immune, who think, '*My pupils*' or '*My daughter won't be interested in that*' ought to think twice. Some children only have to overhear their parents arguing quietly downstairs a couple of nights in a row about something as trivial as the new colour for the kitchen cabinets, to misunderstand and think, with vivid pain, that any day now, they're going to have a problem too. Readers can test themselves against lives they might have to live – when Dad leaves; when the bomb drops; when plague strikes; when the hard men take over; when they fail all their exams. Far from creating insecurities and anxieties, reading seems rather to put the unspoken, but often imagined, worries firmly back into proportion. The reader closes the book and he can't help thinking, '*Well, if a wimp like him can confess to his parents and face the music and live, I probably could too.'*

I think that the children for whom troubled family situations are already a fact need fiction even more. These children can so easily end up torn between two realities. Like us, they don't need to hear the actual words; they can read faces; they can understand the facial tic that means, *'Your father's a pig, he doesn't even pay your child support.'* They understand the shrug that says, *'She's just trying to poison you all against me. She's bitter because she's lost her meal-ticket for life.'* Children can't easily see both sides at the same time as they are watching one parent in tears at the kitchen table, so they tend to draw in their emotional horns, and their understanding. We've all seen it – under stress, a lot of children go seemingly deaf and stupid and detached. But in a book exploring another family's experience, light can be shed sideways on their own. And it's only through being able to see all sides that a child can move away from what is often the parents' real-life fictions into a larger fictional truth and so get on with his or her emotional development. There is nothing more tiresome to be around than the closed, the unfurnished mind. Books offer shafts of light into the prison grey of some people's existences. It might be in a book, for example, that an unthinking bigot first comes across a sustained description of liberal ways of thinking. It might be in a book that a girl who cowers under her teasing or overbearing parents' hand first comes across the portrait of a warm and supportive family man. I don't know the titles of the novels that have changed your own view of the world, or of your role in it, or your aspirations. And you don't need me to remind you of the titles that have shifted the axis of thinking in society. The novel is still, and probably always will be, the best available instrument of ethical enquiry. Here's Minna, ten years old, wondering why her mother won't lend her ten pence to pay her weekly contribution to the class's sponsored elk at the local zoo.

It's not that Mum's mean. She's not. In fact, Gran says she's positively daft with her money. It's just that she disapproves of zoos – hates them, in fact. She says the animals are cramped and miserable and bored silly, and now almost everyone's got a colour telly, there's no excuse for zoos at all, and she won't support them.

'I'm not asking you to build a new east wing for the monkeys,' I said. 'I just want to borrow ten pence elk money off you. That's all. Ten pence isn't going to keep the zoo gates open, is it?'

'I'm sorry,' said Mum, 'I really am, but you know how I feel about zoos, so I can't lend you your elk money.'

'But, Mum, if I haven't got ten pence, I'll be in trouble.'

'I'm sorry, Minna, but the answer's "no".' I must say, I was pretty shocked. Wouldn't you be? Your very own flesh and blood prepared to drop you in the soup like that, rather than lend you a miserable old ten pence? Extraordinary! In fact, so extraordinary that I thought about it all the way to school that morning. I just couldn't help it. I was trying to work out just what it was about the lives of animals in zoos that so offended her. And maybe I did drift off into a bit of a daydream about what it would really feel like to be a gorgeous powerful wild tiger, locked up forever in a small pen and yard no larger than somebody's back garden. And maybe I did make-believe a little that I was a baby chimpanzee chock full of beans and couldn't ever swing any higher or wider than the top of the cage, or the sides of the cage. Maybe I did get thinking really deeply, and slow down walking, and start to drag my feet a bit along

the paving stones, and take my time, wondering,
wondering ... I didn't know I was going to be
that late, did I?

(*Crummy Mummy and Me*)

I cannot tell you how often I've been told that even a tiny
passage like that has set off a fierce impassioned debate over
a family dinner table or in a primary school classroom. Not
just the '*Are zoos wrong for sentient animals?*' debate, but
also whether Minna's mother should have, just this once, put
her daughter's feelings and convenience before her own
principles. They are important questions. No one can avoid
them all the way through their life, and children as young as
seven and eight can think about them and discuss them, not in
abstract terms, perhaps, but using the characters in the story
as models. '*She was just mean!*' '*Oh no, she wasn't! She
probably felt terrible for Minna all day. It's just that she'd
have felt worse for herself and for the animals, for even longer
if she'd given in,*' and on and on and on. It's actually small
wonder that Susan Sontag once said about her own fiction:
'Sometimes I think that the most useful thing that I can do is
increase the sense of the complexity of things.' I think we
could probably all do with a bit more of that, as lame-brained
ideologues keep trying to force us all to lurch one way in life,
or the other. Books make you stop and think.

During the long debate on library funding in Britain a couple
of years ago, Ian Sproat, as the Minister concerned, asked, in
all seriousness, 'Is there still something sufficiently distinctive
about reading as a recreation to justify its being made publicly
available without charge?' I really do not think that I could
have been the only one of those listening to reckon that, if the
man could even ask the question, it was an indication that he
himself clearly hadn't done enough of it to recognise its true
value. But the book does have to be open. And here we come
up against one of the prickly evergreens of literature: does this
book enrich the mind? Or will it coarsen and corrupt the reader?
Should it be on the shelf or not? Is there an argument for keeping

this book, at least, quite firmly shut? The children's writer, in particular, picks his or her way through a minefield here. And it doesn't seem to help that the mines are set by people with the very best of intentions. None of us wants the people around us to be brought up warped or diminished, but the trouble is that everyone in the whole world is an expert on what other people, particularly children, need and want. We are all at one in this respect alone: secretly, we believe that everyone who agrees with us is showing a modicum of common sense, that those who would censor more than we would, or different things, are being extremist and ideological and sometimes downright silly; and everyone that would censor less than we would is being insensitive on what is *really* a very important issue, or allowing the vulnerable to court danger. But a knee-jerk response – if in doubt, if under any pressure at all, best ban the book – is not worthy of people who have a respect for literature or, in the case of librarians, a respect for their profession, or in the case of parents, a respect for children's intelligence. There are far too many people from far too many special interest groups sitting around seemingly hair-triggered to take offence. In the field of young people's reading, I would be the last to claim that the matter is simple. Children are not adults, their books do introduce them to the world and they serve a teaching purpose. And when an adult gives a child a book, some sort of responsibility, some sort of unspoken *imprimatur* is involved in the transaction. A few of the limits are obvious.

To say there should be no censorship of what children read is a nonsense. If any teacher strolled into a classroom at lunchtime to find all the boys huddled around a copy of some sleazy magazine, and all the girls upset and humiliated in a corner, we would expect him or her to act, and act at once, as a censor. But where's the sensible limit? Perhaps the first thing, as we begin tackling this very tricky problem, is to recall Marina Warner's warning from her Reith Lecture, when she reminds us that childhood and adult life are inextricably intertwined:

> Children are not separate from adults, and, unlike Mowgli and Peter Pan, they cannot be kept separate. They cannot lead innocent lives on behalf of adults, like mediaeval hermits maintained at court by libertine kings to pray for them, or like the best china kept in tissue in the cupboard.

Our children hear the news; they watch the telly; their eyes, like ours, fall with horror on the ghastly headlines. Remember Flannery O'Connor: 'Anybody who survives childhood has enough information about life to last them to the end of their days.' And some of our children end up with a very strange view of how the world around them works. Theodore Dalrymple, writing in *The Spectator*, spoke of walking down the corridor in the hospital to which he is attached as a doctor, and overhearing two parents explaining to their four-year-old son that Granny had died. And the boy's response – four years old! 'Was she shot or was she stabbed?' If we cannot protect them, we must help them through, and here, I think, we could bear in mind Frank Flanagan's observation that it is unfortunately 'common for adults to ignore the child's need for a voice to structure the experience of childhood'. This, he says, is what good writers do. 'They structure, explain and evaluate the experience of childhood, and empower the child to come to terms with it. They enable the child to lead a full life.'

So we must be so wary of deciding too soon what it's wrong for others to read. Imagine the impoverished bookshelves of the child raised in the stifling dictates of political correctness – and they can be stifling. You do not need me to run through all the current sensitivities of race and sex and disablement and worries about witches or pigs or little girls going off alone for an afternoon's adventures. You don't need me to make the usual run of jokes about 'Charlie and the Carob Co-operative', and 'Jack and Jill's Job-share', and 'Steel Grey and the Seven Vertically Challenged Persons', and 'Single Parent Goose'. Though the words 'How stupid!' keep springing to my lips about other people's bugbears, I know my own dwelling, if not exactly a glasshouse, has one or two quite vulnerable panes. I have re-shelved books that imply that our planet is hopelessly, irremediably doomed, rather than buy them for my nephews. I have been happy to let ugly and despairing books slip down the back of my children's shelves – out of sight, out of mind. I have worn the parent's hat.

But it's hard for a professional to believe in the official censorship of books; it's far too dangerous. One man's joke is another man's outrage. Simple realism for one woman is, for another woman, unmitigated offence. And with children, there's this perennial complication that a book left on the shelf for a fourteen-year-old will be checked out by an innocent of nine. In short, there will always be fusses, but the one consolation to me is that, extreme or misguided as some of these people may appear to me to be (and they do), I can still believe they mean well. It's just that, generally, they're not really readers by inclination; certainly, they don't seem to understand books and how they work, and they certainly don't understand the reading child.

I have two points to make on this matter: The first is that children are not halfwits, and a reading child reads a lot. Some children read dozens of books a year, others hundreds. If a book were the only book a child were ever going to read, then, yes, it would be important – vital, even – that that particular book had all of the virtues and none of the weakness, and certainly none of the vices. But this is not what happens. A child reads many books, and the more books it reads, the less impact any one will have, and the more judgement the child will bring to what it reads.

If I may give you an example from personal experience: my own younger daughter was, at the age of eight, not a reader. Oh, she could read, but she didn't, not often. She spent hours on her hand-held computer games, and she made things, and she rode her bike. She was, as it happens, educated in an American kindergarten and elementary school, and there, the textbooks had all been rewritten to show girls poring over engines and boys counting up buttons. There had been, throughout California, a concerted effort to eradicate institutionalised sexism from the school system. We came back to Britain and visited my mother, who promptly handed me three cartons of my old Enid Blyton books. 'Here,' she said, 'take them or they go to the jumble sale.' Now, Enid Blyton is not exactly what a mother, who sees herself as as much on the front line of feminism as the next man, wants to take home to a houseful of impressionable daughters! But I really did love these books when I was young, and I could never have let them go for jumble. So they were stacked on the back seat of the car and we set off for home in Edinburgh. And all the way up the M1 and the M6, and the A74, and the M8, we could hear this bitter little eight-year-old voice spluttering and muttering from the back seat. 'Of course the boys are going through the hedge first ... of course ... of course it's the girls that are crying ... of course ... of course it's the girls who have to make the sandwiches ... of course ... of course it's the boys who get to fetch the boat.' By the time we reached home, my daughter was spitting poison with Enid Blyton's sexism, and she was on her *sixth* book. And from that day to this, my daughter has been the most passionate reader.

So my point here is that books for children are like sex for adults. It is a mystery what turns people on. One is ill-advised to import too strict amorality into children's books. I am quite proud to have written *Bill's New Frock*, a comedy about unwitting sexism in the primary school, but it is simply a fact that one of our most unthinkingly sexist writers was, I have absolutely no doubt, the driving force behind both my becoming a professional writer and my daughter becoming a passionate reader. It's unpalatable for the ideologues among us, but it's true.

My second point is a reminder. It seems to me that professionals nowadays are all too easily persuaded, and sometimes even intimidated, into rushing in and filling one another's roles. The librarian's job is the provision of books – not perfect mental health for all, or ideal social attitudes. Librarians should not be bullied, or shamed, or manipulated into rolling over and playing dead because phrases like 'the children's safety must be paramount' or 'unpleasant racist and sexist attitudes' have such a ring to them. Our libraries are a public service and for librarians to forget their principal role is a serious matter. The protection of children is, of course, an important issue, but it is also a remarkably emotive one. Until generally and publicly agreed otherwise, I think, for the librarian, it should be the provision of books that is the paramount consideration.

But we do actually have to face it: there are plenty enough books available that spend far too little time off the shelves and actually open. This is, I suspect, the one thing of which professional writers are, to their regular mortification, more aware than any other group in the world: how many closed books there are, and how very many people there seem to be who don't come in contact with books at all, would probably never notice if every last one of them disappeared in a puff of smoke, and certainly never would be caught dead sitting in front of one open. I think a lot of us can guess where a lot of these people's time is going. One small, but frightening, statistic should suffice here. Since the first episode of *Coronation Street* was shown in Britain over thirty years ago, viewers have spent a cumulative total of well over four and a half million years watching it. That is an awful lot of people who could have read through *War and Peace*; that is a huge number who would have finished *A Portrait of the Artist as a Young Man*, and moved on to *Ulysses*. On the bright side, Thackeray currently sells twice as many copies a year of *Vanity Fair* as he did at any point in his lifetime, and these can't all be people taking exams. What seems most extraordinary is how much simple pleasure is being missed here. Fiction's sheer power to enchant is never failing, and 'tell me a story' is a perennial plea. Listen to Deborah Moggach on William – Richmal Crompton's *William*:

> He was the sort of brother I never had. Secretly though, I knew he was simply me, but much more fun. He supplied far more fertile imagination than my own, and all the right ideas. He was my first imaginary friend. Alongside my own life existed his: his red-brick house; his boring parents; Ethel, his snooty sister; and Robert, his nervy and insecure older brother. He was the first person to emerge from a book and accompany me; the first to make me realise that fiction is immortal.

You can hear the fervour in this, and you wonder of what does it remind us? And then you think, of course, 'Chimborazo, Cotopaxi took me by the hand ...'

So, open books in front of everyone! It's a worthy ambition, not to be sneezed at by all those who should know better, who go around saying things like, 'I'm afraid I don't find much time for reading nowadays,' or 'I'm not a reading man, myself.' We should remember Jane Austen:

> Oh, it's only a novel, only some work in which the greatest powers of the mind are displayed, in which the most thorough knowledge of human nature, the happiest delineation of its varieties, the liveliest diffusions of wit and humour, are conveyed to the world in the best chosen language.

We shouldn't, any of us – not any of us – miss a trick at getting the right book into the right person's hand, at the right time, whoever they are – even those people about whom we might mistakenly think, 'books aren't what they need most.' Dickens, for example, has no doubt at all that it is only the arts that stand between ourselves and disaster. Listen to him exhorting the readers of *Hard Times*:

> The poor you will always have with you. Cultivate in them, while there is yet time, the utmost graces of the fancies and affections to adorn their lives, so much in need of ornament, or, in the day of your triumph, when romance is utterly driven out of their souls, and they and a bare existence stand face-to-face, reality will take a wolfish turn and make an end of you.

It's a dire warning with which to end my exhortation, so it's over to all of you now, to open all those books and to pass them around. George Eliot said that:

> ... art is the nearest thing to life, and its ultimate aim is to re-shape the human consciousness, and, with it, the structure of society.

And perhaps she's right. Perhaps, if everyone plays their part, maybe all human consciousness could be reshaped, and the structure of society ineffably altered for the better.

1997

THEME

TOWARDS A PHILOSOPHY OF ABSENCE

SPEAKER

John O'Donohue

Philosopher, poet,
best-selling writer on Celtic spirituality

John O'Donohue

Absence is something that I've thought about for a long time.
It is a beautiful theme. There seems to be very little written on
it, and the more I thought about it, the more I became aware of
how many dimensions of our lives it actually touches. I'd like
to begin the lecture by trying to locate the first experience of
absence in some primal kind of moment.

When each of us was born, we became present to the earth
and we entered into an ancient narrative of presence that
preceded us by hundreds and thousands of millions of years. I
think that the first experience that the earth had of real absence
was when the human mind first emerged. That must have been
an amazing experience for the actual earth itself. It had, up to
then, created incredible masterpieces. If you ever see a twilight,
with the incredible nuance and depth of colour that it has; if
you look at the amazing choruses of waves that beat against a
shoreline; if you look at the mystical shape of mountains, the
voice of streams and rivers and the undomesticatable wildness
of certain wilderness places, you will know that the imagination
of the earth had created great beauty.

I always think that absence is the sister of presence; that the
opposite of presence isn't absence, but vacancy. Vacancy is a
neutral, indifferent, inane, blank kind of space, whereas absence
has real energy; it has a vitality in it, and it is infused with
longing. Sometimes a great way to come to know a word is to
go back to its roots. If you go back to the roots of the word
'absence', you find that it is rooted in Latin – *ab esse* – to be
elsewhere. To be absent is to be away from a person, or a
place; it is an act of departure from your expected and natural
belonging. So all absence holds the echo of some fractured

intimacy, but the intimacy came first, and then, when it was broken, the absence filled the heart. The most common experience of absence is when you lose a friend who is close to you. This indicates the regions of absence that people every human life. When you open yourself to the activity and sacrament of friendship with someone, you create a unique and particular kind of space with them; a special space that you share in the same way with no one else. And when the friend departs – when a relationship breaks or when you lose someone in that final severance that we call death – absence haunts your heart and makes your belonging sore and painful. In some way, there is still within you some kind of innocence that is either unable or unwilling to accept that the person has finally gone and forever. So absence is never clear-cut. Everyone that leaves your life leaves a subtle trail of connection with you. And when you think of them, and miss them and desire them, your heart journeys out again along that trail towards them in the elsewhere that they now find themselves.

Physically considered, we are all objects; we are physical bodily objects. But considered in terms of affection, affectively, there is a myriad secret pathways that go out from every heart. They go out to the earth, they go out to intimate places, they go out to the past. And they go out particularly towards the friends that are really close to us.

When I was preparing this talk, I was looking back along the old tradition to see if there were any ancient Irish stories about absence, and I came upon the beautiful legend of Midhir and Etáin. The fairy prince Midhir fell in love with Etáin, and his wife, Fuamnach, was very jealous, so, with the help of a druid, she changed Etáin into a butterfly, and then, to add more fury, she set a terrible storm going, which blew Etáin all through the country for seven years, until she finally landed at the palace of Aengus, the god of love. He recognised her even though she was a butterfly, took her in, built invisible walls around her, and gave her a beautiful garden. During the night, she came back to the form of a woman, and during the day she was a butterfly. But Fuamnach, Midhir's husband, found out about it and chased her again with a storm, until she landed again in another palace and fell into the goblet of the queen as she was drinking wine. The queen drank her down, and she was reborn nine months later as a beautiful child, whom they, unknowingly, called Etáin again. All the time, the lover Midhir longed for her, searched every corner of the country, and couldn't find her. Then she grew up to be a beautiful woman and the king of Tara, the High King of Ireland, took her as his wife.

One day, at the great gathering, the great assembly in Tara, Midhir recognised her as the one his heart had so hungered for, and whose absence had haunted him. He invited her to go back with him, but she didn't recognise him, because her last metamorphosis had erased her memory completely. He then played the king in a game of chess and he won. He asked that, for his winning, he be allowed to receive one kiss from Etáin. He met her, and when she heard that – the king didn't let him kiss her for a long time –some knowing within her was kindled again, and she began to dream of her former life. Little by little, she began to recall all that she had forgotten and, as she did, her love for Midhir returned totally. When he came back to kiss her, the king had an army around not to let him in, but, magically, he appeared in the middle of the assembly hall and embraced her. The king came to attack them and they weren't there. When the king's men went outside, they looked up and there were two white swans circling in the starry heavens above the palace.

It's a beautiful story to show how, when love or friendship happens, a distinctively unique tone is struck, a unique space is created, and the loss of this is a haunting absence. The faithfulness of the absence kept Midhir on the quest until he eventually rediscovered her, awoke the absence in her again, and then the two of them become present as swans, ironically in the air element that had created the distance and had created the torture for her.

I believe that the death of every animal and every person creates a kind of an invisible ruin in the world, and that, as the world gets older, it becomes more full with these invisible ruins of vanished presence. Emily Dickinson puts it beautifully when she says:

> Absence disembodies;
> so does Death,
> hiding individuals from the Earth.

It is exactly that act of hiding that causes absence. We are so vulnerable to absence because we desire presence so deeply. One of the deepest longings of the human heart is for real presence. Real presence is the goal of truth, the ideal of love, and the intentionality of prayer here and in the beatific vision in the hereafter. Real presence is the heart of the incarnation and it's also the heart of the Eucharist. This is where imagination works so beautifully with the absences and emptinesses of life. It always tries to find a shape of words or music or colour or stone that will in some way incarnate new presence to fill the absence. I remember once in Venice, during an amazing music festival, I attended an outdoor concert in Piazza San Marco, with Stravinsky's music and a ballet, and the moon was full and the sea was wild. There were certain moments in that concert when moon and ocean and dance and music and audience congealed into one pulse – an amazing experience of unity, and, in some strange way, a breakthrough to real presence. When we experience real presence, we break through to that which is latently in us, that is eternal, but which the normal daily round of life keeps distant from us.

The social world is usually governed by a sophisticated and very intricate grammar of absence. You think of the work you do and the people you work with. You think of people who do work that you wouldn't like, people who have to hit the one bolt every twenty seconds for a full day. There's no way that you could do that, unless, of course, you were a saint or a Zen mystic, with real intention. The only way you can do it is by somehow being in conditioned reflex and being actually absent and away elsewhere. That is what I think Karl Marx had in mind when he talked about alienation; in some sense there are certain kinds of functions which diminish and empty our own self-presence and make us absent to our own lives. To do these things continuously in this divided way brings us far away from who we are and from what we are called to do here. That is *real* alienation.

Of course, sometimes it's lovely to be absent from things. I am reminded of a writer who, in describing a character, said, 'He has quite a good presence, but a perfectly delightful absence.' In other words, when he wasn't around, happiness increased in some way. There's a lovely Palestinian American poet that I like, called Naomi Shihab Nye, who has a wonderful poem called 'The Art of Disappearing' that I'd like to read.

When they say, 'Don't I know you?'
say 'No.'

When they invite you to the party,
remember what parties are like
before answering.
Someone telling you in a loud voice
they once wrote a poem.
Greasy sausage balls on a paper plate.
Then reply.

If they say, 'We should get together,'
say, 'Why?'

It's not that you don't love them any more.
You're trying to remember something
too important to forget.
Trees. The monastery bell at twilight.

Tell them you have a new project.
It will never be finished.

When someone recognises you in a grocery store,
Nod briefly and become a cabbage.
When someone you haven't seen in ten years
appears at the door,
Don't start singing him all your new songs.
You will never catch up.

Walk around feeling like a leaf.
Know you could tumble any second.
Then decide what to do with your time.

The art of disappearing certainly has its own kind of value. In a strange way, in modern society we seem to be inhabiting the world of absence more than presence through the whole world of technology and virtual reality. Very often it seems that the driven nature of contemporary society is turning us into the ultimate harvesters of absence, that is, ghosts in our own lives.

In post-modern culture, the mind is particularly homeless, haunted by a sense of absence that it can neither understand nor transfigure. Many of the traditional shelters have fallen down. Religion seems more and more, certainly in its official presentation, to speak in an idiom that is unable to converse with the modern spiritual hunger. Politics seems devoid of vision and is becoming more and more synonymous with economics. Consumerist culture worships accumulation and power, and creates, with incredible arrogance, its own hollow and gaudy hierarchies. In this country, in our admiration for the achievement and velocity of the Celtic Tiger, we are refusing to notice the paw-marks of its ravages and the unglamorous remains of its prey.

Our time is often filled up with forced presence, every minute filled out with something, but every minute merely an instant, lacking the patience and mystery of continuity that awakens that which is eternal within time. Sometimes, when people in a society are unable to read or decipher the labyrinth of absence, their homeless minds revert to nostalgia. They see the present as a massive fall from a once glorious past, where perfect morality, pure faith and impeccable family values pertained, without critique or alternative or any smudge of complexity or unhappiness. All fundamentalism is based both on faulty perception and on unreal nostalgia. What is created is a fake absence in relation to the past. It is used to look away from the challenge and potential of the present and to create a future which is meant to resemble a past that never actually existed. It is very sad, sometimes, to see the way a grid of a certain kind of language can form over a person's spirit and hold them completely trapped and transfixed in a very stiff ideological position. It happens an awful lot in religion. Sometimes, a grid of dead religious language blocks the natural pores of people's spirit. Blind faith is meant to be ultimate sanctity, but it is merely an exercise in absence that keeps you away from that which is truly your own, and keeps you outside the magic and playfulness and dangerous otherness of divinity.

As we journey onwards in our lives, we seem to accumulate more and more absences. This is very marked in relation to old people; their most intimate friends are usually in the unseen world among the dead. But any life that is vigorous and open to challenge and compassion and the real activity of thought knows that, as we journey, we create many tabernacles of absence within us.

Yet, there is a place where our vanished days secretly gather. Memory, as a kingdom, is full of the ruins of presence. It is fascinating that, in your memory, nothing is lost or ever finally forgotten. We all have had experience of this. Sometimes the needle of thought finds its way into a groove of memory and suddenly an old experience that you no longer remembered comes back almost pure and fresh and intact to you. So memory is the place where absence is transfigured and where our time in the world is secretly held for us. As we grow older, our bodies diminish, but our minds and our memories grow more intense.

Yet our culture is very amnesiac. And amnesia is an incredible thing. Imagine if – God between us and all harm – you had an accident and you lost your memory completely. You wouldn't know who you were, where you were, or who you were with. So, in a certain sense, memory keeps presence alive and is always bringing out of what seemed to be absent new forms of presence.

There is another level of absence as well, and it is that which has not vanished, but that which has not yet arrived. We all live in a pathway in the middle of time, so there are lots of events, people, places, thoughts, experiences still ahead of us that haven't actually arrived at the door of our hearts at all. This is the world of the unknown. Questions and thinking are ways of reaching into the unknown to find out what kind of treasures it actually holds. The question is the place where the unknown becomes articulate in us. A good question is something that has incredible grace and light and depth to it. A good question is something that always, in some way, ploughs the invisible furrows of absence to find the nourishment and the treasure that we actually need.

This is where the imagination plays a powerful role, because the imagination loves absence rather than presence. Absence is full of possibility and it always brings us back new reports from the unknown that is yet to come towards us. This is especially true in art. Music is *the* art form that most perfectly sculpts and draws out the poignance of the silence between the notes. Really good music has an incredible secret sculpture of silence in it. The wonderful conductor who died several months ago, Georg Solti, said that, towards the end of his life, he was becoming ever more fascinated with the secret presence of silence within music. If you listen to Mozart's *Requiem*, or Wagner's *Overture to Tristan and Isolde*, you'll know the beauty and poignance of absence as expressed in music. Then, if you want to go for something totally different, that amazing man, Lou Reed, recorded an incredible album a few years ago – an album of tormented hymns to friends of his who died of AIDS. It's called *Magic and Loss*, and there you will see absence in an incredibly intense and powerful kind of way.

The imagination is always fascinated by what is absent. The first time you read a short story, it is very frustrating, because the best story is the one that is not told at all. The short story will bring you to a threshold and leave you there, and you'll be dying to know what happened to the character, or how did the story go further. It is not cheating you – it is bringing you to a threshold and inviting you to open the door for yourself, so that you can have a genuinely original and new experience. So the imagination always recognises that the most enthralling aspect of presence is actually that which is omitted. The art of writing a really good poem is to know what to leave out. John McGahern said that, when he has finished a manuscript, he goes back over it and the first pieces that he starts doing surgery on are the pieces that he likes best! He knows that these are the pieces that he can't trust himself with. You gradually sculpt the thing back until you have a slender shape which has lots of holes in it, but in this absence, you give free play to the imagination to fill it out for itself. You respect the dignity and potential of the reader.

The imagination is incredibly important in this respect in contemporary society, because it mirrors the complexity of our souls. Society always reduces everything to a simple common denominator; religion does it, politics does it, the media do it as well. Only the imagination has the willingness to witness to that which is really complex, dark, paradoxical, contradictory and awkward within us, that which doesn't fit comfortably on the veneer of the social surface. So we depend on the imagination to trawl and retrieve our poignant and wounded complexity which has to remain absent from the social surface. The imagination is really the inspired and uncautious priestess who, against the wishes of all systems and structures, insists on celebrating the liturgy of presence at the banished altars of absence. So the imagination is faithful to the full home of the heart, and all its rooms.

Often in country places – probably in the city too – there was a haunted house, which no one would go into and people would pass with great care, especially late at night. I often think that there is, in every life, some haunted room that you'd never want to go into, and that you do your best to forget was there at all. You'll never break in that door with your mind, or with your will. Only with the gentle coaxing of the imagination will that door be opened to you and will you be given the gift back again of a part of yourself that either you or someone else had forced you to drive away and reject on yourself.

If you look at the characters in literature, there are no saints, because saints, in terms of the imagination, are not interesting people. They are too good. The imagination is always interested in where things break down – failure, resentment, defeat, contradiction, bitterness, darkness, glory, light and possibility – the wild side of ourselves that society would rather forget was there at all. So the imagination mirrors and articulates also that constant companion dimension of the heart that, by definition and design, remains perennially absent – the subconscious. All we know of ourselves is just a certain little surface and there's a whole under-earth of complexity to us that, by definition, keeps out of our sight. It is actually absent to us. It comes through dreams. Sometimes it comes very powerfully through crises or through trauma, but the imagination is the presence within us that brings that hidden, netted grounding side of ourselves up to the surface, and can coax it into harmony with our daily self that we actually know. It's amazing how many of your needs and hungers and potential and gifts and blindness are actually rooted in the subconscious side of your life, and most of that great plantation of your subconscious seems to have actually happened in the playfields and innocence of childhood.

Childhood is an amazing forest of mystery. One of the sad things about contemporary society is the way that childhood has been shrunk back and children now only have a few years of natural innocence before the force and the metallic and sophistication of the world is actually in on top of them. It frightens me sometimes to think of the effect that might have on them later on in their lives, because one of the things that keeps you balanced on your journey is the great forest of your childhood that holds everything anchored there for you.

Now, to relate this to the social level, absence works very powerfully here; in other words, media represent society – they are the mirror of society in a way – they have a powerful, colouring influence on the thin and rapid stream of public perception. And yet media are not straight or direct; they are always involved in the act of selectivity – who appears on the news, how the news is structured? And who are the people in our society that we never see? Who are the absent ones that we never hear from? There are many of them, and, when you start thinking about it, they are usually the poor and the vulnerable. We have no idea, those of us who are privileged, of the conditions in which so many poor and underprivileged people actually live. Because it is not our world, we don't actually see it at all. So these people are absent and they are deliberately kept out, because their voices are awkward, they are uncomfortable, and they make us feel very uneasy.

Another kind of absence in life that is very frightening is the sudden absence of health; when illness arrives. Your self-belonging can no longer be spontaneous and you are now invited, in serious illness, to live in a bleak world that you don't know. You have to negotiate and work everything as if you are starting a new kind of life. Those who are mentally insane live in a jungle of symbols where there is only the smallest order, and sometimes, when there are clearings there, and when they see how haunted they are, there must be a feeling and an experience of such awful poignance.

Then there are those who are sentenced to be absent from their homes and from their lives, and these are the prisoners. One of the fears that I always had – even as a child – was the fear that you could be arrested for something that you never did, but that you could never prove that you hadn't actually done it. I've known friends of mine who went to jail for different things, and the force of anonymity that's brought down to unravel your presence and your identity is just unbelievable. There are people who have done awful things, and of course we have to put them away, but the actual experience of prisoners must be terrible. It must be terrible to be living thirty years of your life in Mountjoy Jail. Your one life on the earth. Joseph Brodsky who was in jail said: 'The awful thing about being a prisoner and being in jail is that you have very limited space, and unlimited time.' When you put those two things together, it is an incredible load on the mind.

The other aspect of absence that I'd like to mention in an Irish context is the absence of Irish people from their own country; the massive haemorrhage of emigration that has been happening over decades and over centuries. I remember working in America when I was about nineteen or twenty, meeting an old man from our village at home. He was about eighty-five years of age and had left when he was eighteen and had never gone back. Even though he was physically in America, in his mind he was still in north Clare. He could remember the names of fields, pathways, stones, trees in camera-precise detail. It must be a wrenching thing to have to be absent from your own place in a totally different kind of world. This raises all kinds of economic and political questions.

Then there are those who deliberately choose the way of absence. These are the contemplatives. They are amazing people; they leave behind the whole bustle of the world, and submit their vulnerable minds to the acidic solitude of the contemplative cell. They are called to face outside social absence and the labyrinths of inner absence, and who knows how they civilise and warm the bleak territories of loss and emptiness for the rest of us? I am sure that if you could read the actual soul or psychic arithmetic of the world, it is unknown what evil and destruction and darkness such contemplative prayer transfigures and keeps away from us. Noel Dermot O'Donohue, the wonderful Carmelite mystic from the kingdom of Kerry, says that the contemplatives or the mystics are people who withdraw from the world to confront the monster in its lair. Maybe our tranquillity is an unknown gift from all of those unglamorous absent ones who are called or forced to excavate the salt mines of absence. I feel that we owe them an incredible kind of secret debt. I also think that people who are ill, and who carry illness for decades in rooms that no one goes into – it is unknown the mystical creativity of the work that they actually do.

And finally, to come on to one of the great absences from the world, which everyone complains about, and that is the absence of God. Particularly in our century, with the Holocaust and the World Wars, Yugoslavia and all the rest of it, there's a great cry out against the absence of God. In the 18th century, Hegel said God was dead, and then in the 19th century, Nietzsche took that up; it is an old question. In the classical tradition, theologians were aware of the absence of God as well. There was the notion of the *Deus absconditus*, the absconded or vanished God. One of the points of absolute subversive realism of the Christian story is that Christ came out of the safety of the sky and stood in Calvary against the absolute silence of God and carried the suffering of the world. The Crucifixion is that bleak place where no certainty can ever settle, and the realism of that is incredibly truthful to the depth and power of absence that suffering and pain and oppression bring to the world. And that is what the Eucharist is about; in the Eucharist you have the most amazing symphony of complete presence based on the ultimate absence and the ultimate kind of emptiness. It's fascinating, too, that sometimes absence creates new possibility. When the carpenter rose from the dead, they wanted him to stay around, and he said no, that he must go, in order to let the Spirit come. So sometimes that which is absent allows something new to emerge.

The final absence I want to deal with is the absence that none of us will be finally able to avoid – our own absence from the earth and that will happen to us in death. Death is the ultimate absence. Part of the sadness of contemporary society that has lost its mystical and mythological webbing is that we can no longer converse with the dead, and we're no longer aware of them. The dead are notoriously absent from us. I think that you can characterise your life in different ways. One of the ways is the time before someone that is close to you dies, and the time afterwards. That happened for me when my uncle died and I'd like to read this poem, called *November Questions*, where I tried to trawl the vacancy of his absence for some little glimpse or signal of who he was now, or where he was.

November Questions

Where did you go
when your eyes closed
and you were cloaked
in the ancient cold?

How did we seem,
huddled around
the hospital bed?
Did we loom as
figures do in dream?

As your skin drained,
became vellum,

a splinter of whitethorn
from your battle with a bush
in the Seangharraí
stood out in your thumb.

Did your new feet
take you beyond
to fields of Elysia
or did you come back
along Caherbeanna mountain
where every rock
knows your step?

Did you have to go
to a place unknown?
Were there friendly faces
to welcome you,
help you settle in?

Did you recognise anyone?

Did it take long
to lose
the web of scent,
the honey smell of old hay,
the whiff of wild mint
and the wet odour of the earth
you turned every spring?

Did sounds become
unlinked,
the bellow of cows
let into fresh winterage
the purr of a stray breeze
over the Coillín,
the ring of the galvanised bucket
that fed the hens,

the clink of limestone
loose over a scailp
in the Ciorcán?

Did you miss
the delight of your gaze
at the end of a day's work
over a black garden,
a new wall
or a field cleared of rock?

Have you someone there
that you can talk to,
someone who is drawn
to the life you carry

With your new eyes
can you see from within?
Is it we who seem
outside?

There is one force that pervades both presence and absence, can't be located particularly anywhere, and can be subtracted from nowhere, and that force is spirit. We talk of absence and space, and absence and time, but we can never talk about the absence of spirit, because spirit, by nature and definition, can never be absent. So, all space is spiritual space, and in spiritual space there is no real distance. And this raises the question I would like to end with – a fascinating question: while we are here in the world, where is it that we are absent from?

1998

THEME

TOWARDS PEACE IN NORTHERN IRELAND

SPEAKER

George J Mitchell

*Former United States Senator for Maine
and Majority Leader, United States Senate,
Chairman, Multiparty Peace Negotiations
in Northern Ireland,
Special Advisor to the President of the United States
on Economic Initiatives in Ireland*

George J Mitchell

I've been made to feel very much at home here in Cork today and, in a real sense, I am at home. It was just a hundred years ago that a young couple named Kilroy left Cork with their children to go to America. They were part of the human tide which flowed west across the Atlantic and which formed the bonds of blood that ever since have so tightly bound our two countries together. As did many others of their time, they settled in Boston, and there, in the year 1900, their youngest son, Joseph Kilroy, was born. He was my father. Unfortunately, he never knew his parents. His mother died shortly after his birth; his father apparently couldn't care for the children and so they were all placed in orphanages. My father was raised in an orphanage in Boston, and ultimately adopted by an elderly couple, named Mitchell, who settled in a small town in the state of Maine. There he met my mother who, at the age of eighteen, had left her native Lebanon and emigrated to the United States.

Neither of my parents had any education – my mother could not read or write English – and they worked all of their lives at difficult and low-paying jobs. But, because of their efforts, because I received so many helping hands along the way, and because of the openness of American society, of which I, an American, am deeply proud, I, their son, was able to become the Majority Leader of the United States Senate. Although my father was not an educated man, he was a wise man. He taught me many things, more by example than by words, but a few words he said to me are relevant to my experience here in Ireland. He told me, as I left our home to go to college, that he wanted me to succeed and that, although he could do little to help me succeed, he would do all he could. But most of all he wanted me to remember that if, by the grace of God, I were able to succeed, I would have a lifelong obligation to help others, 'an obligation,' he said, 'which you can never extinguish and which you must always act in accordance with.' Those words were in my mind many years later when the prime ministers of Britain and Ireland called me and asked me to serve as chairman of the peace negotiations in Northern Ireland.

I had been in Northern Ireland for about a year and half before that as President Clinton's special advisor and then as chairman of the International Body on Decommissioning. I had begun, over that time, to get to know the people of Northern Ireland. I have since come to know them very well. I like them. I admire them. They deserve better than they've had during the Troubles. They are warm and generous, energetic and productive. They are also, as I remind them, quarrelsome and argumentative, and they have a way with words, but, at bottom, they are truly wonderful people and nothing will please me more than to see a durable peace in Northern Ireland.

A decade earlier, at a time when I had never visited Ireland, north or south, and knew little of the problems here, the governments of Ireland and Britain had come to realise that, if there ever was to be an end to the conflict in Northern Ireland, it had to begin with co-operation by the governments themselves. In 1983, the then Taoiseach, Garret FitzGerald, established what he called the New Ireland Forum, which brought together the main political parties of Ireland and the Social, Democratic and Labour Party (SDLP) of Northern Ireland in an effort to define what the Taoiseach ambitiously called 'A New Ireland'. Their report, issued in 1984, was a major step toward an agreement with the British government, and that agreement was reached a year later, in November of 1985, just thirteen years ago this month. It was called the Anglo-Irish Agreement, and it was a turning point in the history of Northern Ireland because, for the first time, the two governments committed themselves, in writing and irrevocably, to use their best efforts to co-operate to bring about a solution there and to improve relations overall. Dr FitzGerald is here this evening. You were all kind enough to applaud me as I was introduced, for my efforts at the end of the process. I ask you to join me in applauding Dr FitzGerald for his efforts, which began the process.

It took eleven years and many setbacks before peace negotiations finally began that would bring about a successful conclusion. There was, in the interim, a negotiation in 1991 and 1992 which did not produce agreement. There was the Downing Street Declaration of December 1993, by the then Taoiseach, Albert Reynolds and the British Prime Minister, John Major, which represented a huge step forward, seeking, as it did, to reconcile the conflicting views of the two governments on the constitutional status of Northern Ireland, and also seeking to answer the question of how those political parties which were associated with paramilitary organisations could be brought into an inclusive negotiation.

Finally, after many setbacks, and much effort, negotiations began in June of 1996. It was by far the most difficult negotiation with which I have ever been involved. Almost two years passed before agreement was reached and, during that time, there was, for the most part, little progress and little hope of progress. But the governments persevered and the newly-elected British Labour government, led by Tony Blair, and the newly-elected Irish government in June of 1997, led by Bertie Ahern, provided the final impetus to bring about a successful conclusion.

Many people deserve credit for the agreement, but I think ultimately it is the people of Northern Ireland and their political leaders who deserve that credit. The political leaders of Northern Ireland have been much maligned and harshly criticised, here in the Republic, in Northern Ireland and in other parts of the United Kingdom. But they are men and women of substance and courage and, in exceptionally difficult circumstances, risking not just their political careers, but their very lives and the safety of their families, they came together to find common ground in an agreement which, while imperfect, in my judgement will endure. It will endure because it is fair and balanced; it reflects a true, principled compromise and, most importantly, commits all of the participants to the total disarmament of all paramilitary organisations, and to the use of exclusively democratic and peaceful means to resolve their political differences.

It must be clear and acknowledged and repeated that the Good Friday Agreement does not, by itself, guarantee or provide peace, political stability and reconciliation in Northern Ireland; it makes them possible. But if they are to be achieved, many difficult decisions lie ahead. There will be setbacks, and much courage remains to be demonstrated by the political leaders of Northern Ireland and by the two governments. But I am convinced that it will endure, primarily because of the overwhelming endorsement of the people of Ireland, north and south, in a free and open democratic election, held in May of this year. Of all of the wise steps taken by the governments to create and sustain this process, none, in my judgement, was wiser than their decision to subject any agreement to a referendum, to ensure that it would not be just the work of politicians, but it would indeed be the work of the people themselves.

Reconciliation, genuine reconciliation will be much harder to come by and will take much longer. A few years ago, while I was serving as Majority Leader of the United States Senate, I paid one of many visits to a war-torn region in the north of Bosnia, along the Bosnia-Croatian border. I visited a small town there which, before the war, had been occupied by a population of about half Serbs and half Croats. When the war began, the Serbs gained the military advantage, took control of the town and drove all of the Croats away. The Serbs then burned down every building in the town that was owned by a Croat.

The tides of war changed. Two years later, the Croats regained control of the town and, in retaliation, they burned down every building owned by a Serb.

When I visited, every single building in the village had been destroyed and I observed to the mayor who guided me through the town that it was difficult for an outsider to tell who had won. I then asked the mayor: 'How long will it be before the people of this town, Serbs and Croats, can again live together, side by side?' He was a thoughtful young man and, after a long pause, he replied: 'We will repair our buildings long before we will repair our souls.' A bombed building can be rebuilt, a burnt-out car can be replaced, but what is really difficult is to change what is in people's hearts and minds.

I believe that the most important aspect of the Good Friday Agreement is the emphasis it places on mutual respect and tolerance, on validating and legitimising the different aspirations of the two communities there, and committing them to work with each other in a peaceful and democratic way.

I think it will eventually be the children of Northern Ireland who will bring about genuine reconciliation; children who have not lived through the difficult times of the past, when each new grievance brought a renewal of hatred and a thirst for revenge.

I regard my work there as the most significant thing I have done in my public life, although I am proud of the legislative record I accomplished in the United States Senate, and I believe with all of my heart and soul that this agreement will endure.

I will be going to Belfast tomorrow, where I will be meeting with most of the political leaders, and my message to them will be simple: 'You have come this far, much too far to let this opportunity slip from your grasp.' And the people of this island, north and south, have made it very clear what it is they want. When the people of Ireland voted on May 22nd 1998, they voted for peace over war; they voted for tolerance over sectarian hatred; they voted for the future over the past. The bonds of history are important; they are what create and bind a society together. But unless the people of Northern Ireland want history to repeat itself in the future, then they must break the chains of the past and look to the future, look to a future of opportunity and, I believe, tremendous prosperity.

I want to close with a couple of personal anecdotes. Throughout the nearly two years of the negotiations, there was constant speculation by the media that I would leave, out of frustration and disgust at the lack of progress. Indeed, almost every time I faced the press in Northern Ireland, the very first question was: 'Senator, when are you leaving?' For a while I got the feeling that some of them wanted me to go, but I accepted the legitimacy of the question. I will confess to you that I often thought of leaving, and especially in the spring of 1997 when we had a lengthy break in the negotiations for elections held in the British Parliament, and then District and Local Councils in Northern Ireland. Things looked very difficult, and the prospects were slim. I discussed with my wife and friends of mine the possibility of leaving, and that was much on my mind throughout that summer and early fall.

And then, on October 16th of 1997, a transforming event occurred in my life: my wife gave birth to our son. Every parent here knows what that means. In my case, it involved more than personal feelings; it involved my role in Northern Ireland. On the day that my son was born, I telephoned my staff in Belfast and asked them to find out how many babies had been born in Northern Ireland on that day. There were sixty-one. And I became seized with the thought: what would life be like for my son had he been born in Northern Ireland? What would life be like for those sixty-one babies, had they been born Americans?

The aspirations of parents everywhere are the same: to have children who are healthy and happy, safe and secure, who get a good education and a good start in life, who have the chance to go as high and as far as talent and willingness to work will take them.

A few days after my son's birth, in what was, for me, a very painful parting, I left home to return to Belfast, to resume chairing the negotiations, and on that flight, I resolved that I would not leave, no matter what. I committed myself to the end, and promised to redouble my efforts to bring the negotiations to a successful conclusion.

And when I returned to the negotiations the next day, the delegates were very kind and expressed their congratulations on the birth of my son, and I told them of my thoughts. I told them that I was committed to stay until the end, that I was prepared to redouble my efforts, and I asked them for the same commitment. And I reminded them of the high obligation that they had as the elected representatives of the people of Northern Ireland not to let this opportunity pass.

We were able to bring it to a successful conclusion, thanks to their courage and perseverance. After the agreement was reached, on Good Friday this year, we came together for one last time. It was very emotional. Everyone was exhausted. We had stayed in negotiating session for nearly forty consecutive hours. For most of the previous two weeks, everyone had gotten little sleep, and so some cried; there were tears of exhaustion, of relief, of joy. I told the delegates, in my parting words, that, for me, the Good Friday Agreement was the realisation of a dream, a dream that had sustained me through three and a half of the most difficult years of my life.

Now, that dream has been realised and I have a new dream. It is this: my dream now is that, in a few years, I will take my young son and return to Northern Ireland. We will tour that beautiful country until, on one rainy afternoon, we'll go to visit the new Northern Ireland Assembly. That won't be difficult, because almost every afternoon is a rainy afternoon! And there we will sit in the visitors' gallery of the Assembly and watch the delegates there debate the ordinary issues of life in a democratic society – healthcare, education, agriculture, fisheries, tourism. There will be no talk of war, for the war will have long been over. There will be no talk of peace, for peace will be taken for granted. On that day, the day on which peace is taken for granted in Northern Ireland, on that day I will be truly fulfilled.